# Learning Internet of Things

Explore and learn about Internet of Things with the help of engaging and enlightening tutorials designed for Raspberry Pi

**Peter Waher**

BIRMINGHAM - MUMBAI

# Learning Internet of Things

Copyright © 2015 Packt Publishing

All rights reserved. No part of this book may be reproduced, stored in a retrieval system, or transmitted in any form or by any means, without the prior written permission of the publisher, except in the case of brief quotations embedded in critical articles or reviews.

Every effort has been made in the preparation of this book to ensure the accuracy of the information presented. However, the information contained in this book is sold without warranty, either express or implied. Neither the author, nor Packt Publishing, and its dealers and distributors will be held liable for any damages caused or alleged to be caused directly or indirectly by this book.

Packt Publishing has endeavored to provide trademark information about all of the companies and products mentioned in this book by the appropriate use of capitals. However, Packt Publishing cannot guarantee the accuracy of this information.

First published: January 2015

Production reference: 1210115

Published by Packt Publishing Ltd.
Livery Place
35 Livery Street
Birmingham B3 2PB, UK.

ISBN 978-1-78355-353-2

www.packtpub.com

# Credits

**Author**
Peter Waher

**Reviewers**
Fiore Basile
Dominique Guinard
Phodal Huang
Joachim Lindborg
Ilesh Patel

**Commissioning Editor**
Akram Hussain

**Acquisition Editors**
Richard Brookes-Bland
Richard Harvey

**Content Development Editor**
Anila Vincent

**Technical Editor**
Anushree Arun Tendulkar

**Copy Editors**
Gladson Monteiro
Jasmine Nadar

**Project Coordinator**
Neha Bhatnagar

**Proofreaders**
Ameesha Green
Amy Johnson

**Indexer**
Hemangini Bari

**Graphics**
Sheetal Aute
Valentina D'silva

**Production Coordinator**
Manu Joseph

**Cover Work**
Manu Joseph

# About the Author

**Peter Waher** is the cofounder of Clayster, a company with its origin in Scandinavia but now operates in four continents. Clayster is dedicated to the development of Internet of Things applications and provides an IoT platform for rapid application development. Currently, Peter lives and works in Chile where he is the CEO of Clayster Laboratorios Chile S.A., a subsidiary of Clayster that provides development expertise to partner companies and promotes the Internet of Things technology to research institutions. Originally a mathematician, commercial pilot, and computer games developer, he has worked for 20 years with computers and device communication, including low-level development in assembler for resource-constrained devices to high-level system design and architecture. He's currently participating in various standardization efforts within IEEE, UPnP, and XSF, working on designing standards for Internet of Things. His work on smart applications for Internet of Things and the development of the IP-TV application "Energy Saving through Smart Applications" won the Urban Living Labs global showcase award in the Cultural and Societal Participation and Collaboration Tools category. Peter Waher can be found on LinkedIn at `http://linkedin.com/in/peterwaher/`.

> I'd like to thank the founder of Clayster, Rikard Strid, and Packt Publishing for the opportunity to write this book; Joachim Lindborg for the many ideas and discussions related to Internet of Things; Fernando Cruz and Freddy Jimenez for their invaluable help with many practical details; my eldest daughter, Maria-Lorena, for accepting to stand model and offer to break into my office at night; and finally my wife and children for tolerating the many late hours it took to write this book.

# About the Reviewers

**Fiore Basile** is a programmer, system administrator, creative, entrepreneur and maker. Since 1996, he has served as project manager, consultant, and technology officer in industrial and research projects of many sizes across Italy and Europe. He worked in the fields of cultural heritage, e-health, digital preservation, multimodal interfaces, web and mobile publishing. During his career, he also founded two IT start-ups, held workshops at international conferences and events, and has been interviewed by national and international press. His work experience allowed him to build a broad expertise in systems, web and mobile software development, open source and open hardware, embedded programming, and electronics. He's currently conducting research on wearable technologies, effective computing, and smart connected devices, and he is working as the coordinator of FabLab Cascina, a digital fabrication laboratory in the middle of Tuscany.

**Dominique "Dom" Guinard** is the CTO and cofounder of EVRYTHNG, a Web of Things and Internet of Things software company that makes products smart by connecting them to the Web. Dom got his PhD from ETH Zurich where he worked on defining the Web of Things architecture, a worldwide network of interconnected objects (sensor networks, appliances, machines, and tagged objects). He also cofounded `WebofThings.org` and the Web of Things conference series.

Before this, he worked on bringing industrial networks of RFID-tagged objects and smart things to the Web at the MIT Auto-ID Labs and was a visiting researcher at the MIT Mobile Experience Lab. He also worked for 4 years with SAP on designing scalable software architectures and infrastructures to integrate real-world objects with business systems. Dom was a researcher at the Auto-ID Labs, Zurich, where he worked on using mobile phones as gateways to Internet of Things (IoT) for Nokia. Before this, he worked on scalable IoT enterprise software architectures for RFID and embedded devices in collaboration with Sun Microsystems.

He holds an MSc degree in computer science and a BSc in computer science and management with a specialization in mobile and ubiquitous computing. In 2011, Dominique was listed fifth among the world's top 100 IoT thinkers. Early in 2012, his PhD research on the Web of Things was awarded the ETH Medal.

**Phodal Huang** has over 4 years of experience in hardware and web development. He graduated from Xi'an University of Arts and Science. He currently works at ThoughtWorks as a developer. He is the owner of the mini IoT project (`https://github.com/phodal/iot`) and the author of the eBook, *Design IoT* (`http://designiot.phodal.com`, in Chinese). He loves designing, painting, writing, traveling, and hacking; you can find out more about him on his personal website at `http://www.phodal.com`.

**Joachim Lindborg** is a dedicated systems engineer with a long experience of all the technologies that have been passed through the years, starting from Texas Instrument TI-16 to deploying Docker components on Core-Os on a distributed network of Intel NUC machines.

He is deeply into the exploding area of small devices. Electronics has always been fascinating and Joachim started soldering electronics in seventh grade. The Raspberry explosion with open hardware and software and MakerSpace enthusiasm is a revival and reclaim from the big producers.

Joachim's current focus is to combine these different forms of knowledge of large systems and hardware with meters and actuators to create smart energy services.

Starting in 1993, Joachim was part of the biggest telecom project in Ericsson. The project aimed at creating the next century telecom platforms, ATM. TCP/IP seems to be the winner. For his next big project, he was at the Swedish Utility for several years, building smart home services, which was a pre-millennium shift as they were using phone lines and modems. This is a dead technology now.

It was really in 2002, when Joachim was one of the founders of `homesolutions.se.loopiadns.com`, that his system architect skills were used to create a distributed Linux system. Today, this system has some 46,000 apartments that measure electricity, water, and so on, and create advanced building automation.

In his current assignment as the CTO for sustainable innovation, there is a constant need for IoT-distributed logic and advanced data analyses to gain energy efficiency and a sustainable society.

He has also contributed to a Swedish IT architect book, `http://www.thearchitectbook.com/`.


**Ilesh Patel** holds a bachelor's degree in electronics and communication and a master's degree in VLSI and Embedded System Design. He has more than 3 years of experience as an embedded engineer. He has good debugging skills and command over the high-level C/C++ language, the scripting language Python, and the hardware language VHDL. He has knowledge and hands-on experience on how to design and develop an automated test suite framework using Python, Microcontroller, and an FPGA-based system design development.

> I'd like to thank my friend Uchit Vyas for encouraging me to review this book.

# www.PacktPub.com

## Support files, eBooks, discount offers, and more

For support files and downloads related to your book, please visit www.PacktPub.com.

Did you know that Packt offers eBook versions of every book published, with PDF and ePub files available? You can upgrade to the eBook version at www.PacktPub.com and as a print book customer, you are entitled to a discount on the eBook copy. Get in touch with us at service@packtpub.com for more details.

At www.PacktPub.com, you can also read a collection of free technical articles, sign up for a range of free newsletters and receive exclusive discounts and offers on Packt books and eBooks.

https://www2.packtpub.com/books/subscription/packtlib

Do you need instant solutions to your IT questions? PacktLib is Packt's online digital book library. Here, you can search, access, and read Packt's entire library of books.

### Why subscribe?

- Fully searchable across every book published by Packt
- Copy and paste, print, and bookmark content
- On demand and accessible via a web browser

### Free access for Packt account holders

If you have an account with Packt at www.PacktPub.com, you can use this to access PacktLib today and view nine entirely free books. Simply use your login credentials for immediate access.

# Table of Contents

**Preface**   **1**

**Chapter 1: Preparing our IoT Projects**   **11**
- **Creating the sensor project**   **12**
  - Preparing Raspberry Pi   13
  - Clayster libraries   14
  - Hardware   15
  - Interacting with our hardware   16
  - Interfacing the hardware   17
  - Internal representation of sensor values   18
  - Persisting data   18
  - External representation of sensor values   19
  - Exporting sensor data   19
- **Creating the actuator project**   **22**
  - Hardware   22
  - Interfacing the hardware   23
- **Creating a controller**   **24**
  - Representing sensor values   25
  - Parsing sensor data   25
  - Calculating control states   26
- **Creating a camera**   **27**
  - Hardware   27
  - Accessing the serial port on Raspberry Pi   29
  - Interfacing the hardware   29
  - Creating persistent default settings   30
  - Adding configurable properties   30
  - Persisting the settings   31
  - Working with the current settings   32

## Table of Contents

| | |
|---|---|
| Initializing the camera | 32 |
| **Summary** | **33** |
| **Chapter 2: The HTTP Protocol** | **35** |
| **HTTP basics** | **36** |
| **Adding HTTP support to the sensor** | **38** |
| Setting up an HTTP server on the sensor | 39 |
| Setting up an HTTPS server on the sensor | 41 |
| Adding a root menu | 42 |
| Displaying measured information in an HTML page | 44 |
| Generating graphics dynamically | 46 |
| Creating sensor data resources | 51 |
| Interpreting the readout request | 52 |
| Testing our data export | 53 |
| User authentication | 53 |
| Adding events for enhanced network performance | 54 |
| **Adding HTTP support to the actuator** | **54** |
| Creating the web services resource | 55 |
| Accessing individual outputs | 56 |
| Collective access to outputs | 57 |
| Accessing the alarm output | 57 |
| Using the test form | 58 |
| Accessing WSDL | 59 |
| Using the REST web service interface | 59 |
| **Adding HTTP support to the controller** | **60** |
| Subscribing to events | 60 |
| Creating the control thread | 62 |
| Controlling the actuator | 63 |
| **Summary** | **64** |
| **Chapter 3: The UPnP Protocol** | **65** |
| **Introducing UPnP** | **65** |
| Providing a service architecture | 66 |
| Documenting device and service capabilities | 66 |
| **Creating a device description document** | **67** |
| Choosing a device type | 68 |
| Being friendly | 69 |
| Providing the device with an identity | 69 |
| Adding icons | 69 |
| Adding references to services | 70 |
| Topping off with a URL to a web presentation page | 71 |

| | |
|---|---|
| **Creating the service description document** | **71** |
| Adding actions | 72 |
| Adding state variables | 72 |
| Adding a unique device name | 73 |
| **Providing a web interface** | **73** |
| **Creating a UPnP interface** | **74** |
| Registering UPnP resources | 75 |
| Replacing placeholders | 76 |
| Adding support for SSDP | 77 |
| Notifying the network | 78 |
| Responding to searches | 79 |
| **Implementing the Still Image service** | **81** |
| Initializing evented state variables | 81 |
| Providing web service properties | 82 |
| Adding service properties | 83 |
| Adding actions | 83 |
| **Using our camera** | **84** |
| Setting up UPnP | 84 |
| Discovering devices and services | 85 |
| Subscribing to events | 86 |
| Receiving events | 86 |
| Executing actions | 87 |
| **Summary** | **88** |
| **Chapter 4: The CoAP Protocol** | **89** |
| **Making HTTP binary** | **90** |
| Finding development tools | 91 |
| **Adding CoAP to our sensor** | **91** |
| Defining our first CoAP resources | 92 |
| Manually triggering an event notification | 93 |
| Registering data readout resources | 94 |
| Returning XML | 95 |
| Returning JSON | 96 |
| Returning plain text | 96 |
| Discovering CoAP resources | 97 |
| Testing our CoAP resources | 98 |
| **Adding CoAP to our actuator** | **98** |
| Defining simple control resources | 99 |
| Parsing the URL in CoAP | 100 |
| Controlling the output using CoAP | 101 |

## Using CoAP in our controller — 102
### Monitoring observable resources — 102
### Receiving notifications — 103
### Performing control actions — 104
## Summary — 105

# Chapter 5: The MQTT Protocol — 107
## Publishing and subscribing — 108
## Adding MQTT support to the sensor — 110
### Controlling the thread life cycle — 110
### Flagging significant events — 111
### Connecting to the MQTT server — 112
### Publishing the content — 113
## Adding MQTT support to the actuator — 115
### Initializing the topic content — 115
### Subscribing to topics — 115
### Receiving the published content — 116
### Decoding and parsing content — 117
## Adding MQTT support to the controller — 118
### Handling events from the sensor — 118
### Decoding and parsing sensor values — 119
### Subscribing to sensor events — 120
### Controlling the actuator — 120
#### Controlling the LED output — 120
#### Controlling the alarm output — 121
## Summary — 123

# Chapter 6: The XMPP Protocol — 125
## XMPP basics — 126
### Federating for global scalability — 126
### Providing a global identity — 127
### Authorizing communication — 128
### Sensing online presence — 128
### Using XML — 129
### Communication patterns — 129
### Extending XMPP — 130
### Connecting to a server — 131
### Provisioning for added security — 132
## Adding XMPP support to a thing — 133
### Connecting to the XMPP network — 133

| | |
|---|---:|
| Monitoring connection state events | 134 |
| Notifying your friends | 135 |
| Handling HTTP requests over XMPP | 135 |
| **Providing an additional layer of security** | **136** |
| The basics of provisioning | 136 |
| Initializing the Thing Registry interface | 138 |
| Registering a thing | 139 |
| Updating a public thing | 140 |
| Claiming a thing | 140 |
| Removing a thing from the registry | 140 |
| Disowning a thing | 141 |
| Initializing the provisioning server interface | 142 |
| Handling friendship recommendations | 142 |
| Handling requests to unfriend somebody | 143 |
| Searching for a provisioning server | 143 |
| Providing registry information | 145 |
| Maintaining a connection | 145 |
| Negotiating friendships | 146 |
| Handling presence subscription requests | 147 |
| Continuing interrupted negotiations | 148 |
| Adding XMPP support to the sensor | 149 |
| Adding a sensor server interface | 149 |
| Updating event subscriptions | 149 |
| Publishing contracts | 150 |
| **Adding XMPP support to the actuator** | **151** |
| Adding a controller server interface | 151 |
| **Adding XMPP support to the camera** | **152** |
| **Adding XMPP support to the controller** | **153** |
| Setting up a sensor client interface | 153 |
|    Subscribing to sensor data | 153 |
|    Handling incoming sensor data | 154 |
| Setting up a controller client interface | 155 |
| Setting up a camera client interface | 157 |
| Fetching the camera image over XMPP | 157 |
| Identifying peer capabilities | 158 |
| Reacting to peer presence | 159 |
| Detecting rule changes | 160 |
| **Connecting it all together** | **161** |
| **Summary** | **162** |

## Chapter 7: Using an IoT Service Platform — 163

### Selecting an IoT platform — 164
### The Clayster platform — 164
Downloading the Clayster platform — 164
Creating a service project — 165
Adding references — 165
Making a Clayster module — 166
Executing the service — 167
Using a package manifest — 167
Executing from Visual Studio — 168
Configuring the Clayster system — 168
Using the management tool — 169
Browsing data sources — 170
### Interfacing our devices using XMPP — 171
Creating a class for our sensor — 172
   Finding the best class — 172
   Subscribing to sensor data — 173
   Interpreting incoming sensor data — 174
Creating a class for our actuator — 175
   Customizing control operations — 175
Creating a class for our camera — 176
### Creating our control application — 176
Understanding rendering — 177
Defining the application class — 178
Initializing the controller — 178
Adding control rules — 179
Understanding application references — 180
Defining brieflets — 180
Displaying a gauge — 181
Displaying a binary signal — 182
Pushing updates to the client — 184
Completing the application — 185
Configuring the application — 186
Viewing the 10-foot interface application — 186
### Summary — 188

## Chapter 8: Creating Protocol Gateways — 189
### Understanding protocol bridging — 190
### Using an abstraction model — 191
### The basics of the Clayster abstraction model — 193
Understanding editable data sources — 193

| | |
|---|---|
| Understanding editable objects | 194 |
| Using common data sources | 195 |
| Overriding key properties and methods | 196 |
|     Controlling structure | 196 |
|     Publishing properties | 197 |
|     Publishing commands | 197 |
| Handling communication with devices | 197 |
|     Reading devices | 198 |
|     Configuring devices | 198 |
| **Understanding the CoAP gateway architecture** | **198** |
| **Summary** | **200** |
| **Chapter 9: Security and Interoperability** | **201** |
| **Understanding the risks** | **201** |
| Reinventing the wheel, but an inverted one | 202 |
| Knowing your neighbor | 203 |
| **Modes of attack** | **203** |
| Denial of Service | 203 |
| Guessing the credentials | 204 |
| Getting access to stored credentials | 204 |
| Man in the middle | 205 |
| Sniffing network communication | 205 |
| Port scanning and web crawling | 206 |
| Search features and wildcards | 207 |
| Breaking ciphers | 207 |
| **Tools for achieving security** | **208** |
| Virtual Private Networks | 208 |
| X.509 certificates and encryption | 209 |
| Authentication of identities | 209 |
| Usernames and passwords | 210 |
| Using message brokers and provisioning servers | 211 |
| Centralization versus decentralization | 211 |
| **The need for interoperability** | **212** |
| Solves complexity | 212 |
| Reduces cost | 212 |
| Allows new kinds of services and reuse of devices | 213 |
| Combining security and interoperability | 213 |
| **Summary** | **214** |
| **Index** | **215** |

# Preface

Internet of Things is one of the current top tech buzzwords. Large corporations value its market in tens of trillions of dollars for the upcoming years, investing billions into research and development. On top of this, there is the plan for the release of tens of billions of connected devices during the same period. So you can see why it is only natural that it causes a lot of buzz.

Despite this, nobody seems to agree on what Internet of Things (IoT) actually is. The only thing people agree on is that whatever it is, it is worth a lot of money. And where there is a lot of money, there is a lot of competition, which in reality means a lot of confusion. To be able to stand out as a superior player, companies invent new buzz words in an attempt to highlight their superior knowledge. In this battle of gaining the reader's attention, the world is now seeing a plethora of new definitions, one better than the other, such as "Internet of Everything," "Web of Things," "Internet of People and Things," and so on. To pour gasoline on fire, there is a constant overlap and confusion of ideas from related terms, such as "Big Data," "Machine-to-Machine," and "Cyber-Physical Systems" to mention a few.

This lack of consensus on what IoT actually is and what it means makes it somewhat difficult to write a book on the subject. Not because the technical aspects are difficult—they are not—but because you need to define what it is you are going to talk about and also what you are not going to talk about. You need to define IoT in a way that is simple, valid, and constructive, while at the same time it should minimize controversy.

# A definition for Internet of Things

To be able to define IoT, let's first look at how the term was coined. Kevin Ashton noted that most data on the Internet was at the time originally entered or captured into the system by human beings. From a system point of view, a human is nothing more than a slow, error-prone, and inefficient router of data that puts limits on quality and quantity of data available and sometimes even dares to interpret data or correct it. As an alternative, it would be more efficient if these systems could connect to sensors that measure these real-world events or properties directly. So, in this vision, systems bypass human intermediaries and connect directly to sensors connected to the Internet to capture real-world data.

The problem with this definition is that it is not a definition at all but a vision, albeit with an important point. If systems can access data captured by sensors directly, of course, the data will be both more abundant and more correct. This was known decades ago and is a field of study in its own right, labeled "sensor networks". What is the real difference between these two? What is the difference between IoT and Big Data, where the efficient storage of huge volumes of data is handled? How does IoT differ from machine-to-machine (M2M) or device-to-device (D2D) communication, where communication between Things is discussed? Or, how does it differ from cyber-physical systems (CPS) that concerns itself with systems that interact with the real world through sensors and actuators? What is the real difference between IoT and the just mentioned fields of study?

Let's, therefore, have a very simple definition and see where it leads us:

 The IoT is what we get when we connect Things, which are not operated by humans, to the Internet.

# Competing definitions

IoT is not the same as sensor networks since Things neither need to be sensors, nor do sensor networks need to be connected to the Internet. Also, IoT is not the same as big data since neither Things are required to capture or generate data, nor do applications need to store the data centrally (in the Cloud) in big data stores. IoT is not part M2M since being on the Internet implies humans can (and want to) access these Things directly too. Furthermore, the latter, as well as CPS, also concern themselves with non-Internet protocols, transport of messages between machines and/or devices in the network, as well as automation, often in closed and controlled environments.

Being connected to the Internet is much more than simple connectivity and message transport. The Internet is open, meaning anybody can add Things to it. It also means they will want Things to interoperate in a loosely coupled manner. The Internet is not only open, but it also is the largest network in the world. It is also the foulest cesspit in the world. Connect something to the Internet, and you can be rest assured that somebody will try to take advantage of it or destroy it if they can, just for the sheer fun of it. Comparing IoT to M2M communication is like assuming that an experiment in a controlled laboratory environment will continue to work even when you let a bunch of 3-year-old kids high on caffeinated beverages enter the laboratory, equipped with hammers and a playful attitude, and promised ice cream if they destroy everything they could see.

While some are concerned that IoT is too limited to include people in the equation, and it invents new terminologies such as Internet of People and Things, this is already included in the definition we just saw where we noted that people are already connected to the Internet via computers when we connect Things. Such a definition is therefore not necessary. Others discuss a Web of Things (WoT), which is a subset of IoT, where communication is limited to web technologies, such as HTTP, browsers, scripting, and so on. This view might stem from equaling the Internet with the World Wide Web (WWW), where access to the Internet is made through browsers and URLs. Even though we will discuss web technologies in this book, we consider web technologies alone too limiting.

There are also misleading definitions that act more like commercial buzz words rather than technological terminology, such as Internet of Everything, promoting the idea of being something more than IoT. But what is included in Internet of Everything that is not already included in IoT? All connectable Things are already included in IoT. Things that cannot be connected directly (air or water), or indirectly (vacuum or happiness) cannot be accessed in Internet of Everything either, just because the name says so. Everything needs a Thing or a Person to connect to the Internet. There are claims that the Internet of Everything includes processes, and such, and would differ in that sense. But, in the definition we just saw, such processes would be simple corollaries and require no new definition.

# Direct consequences

Now that we have a clear definition of IoT, as something we get when we connect Things, not operated by humans, to the Internet, we are ready to begin our study of the subject. The definition includes four important components:

- Connection, which relates to the study of communication protocols

- Things, which relates to the study of sensors, actuators, and controllers, among other Things
- Non-operation by humans relates to provisioning
- The Internet relates to security, including identities, authentication, and authorization, but also to interoperability

This book will introduce all these concepts one at a time using simple and practical examples illustrating how these key concepts can be implemented using the Raspberry Pi platform.

# What this book covers

*Chapter 1, Preparing our IoT Projects*, introduces the projects we will use throughout the book, their basic project structure, our development environment, how to prepare our Raspberry Pi, and how to perform basic input and output operations on it.

*Chapter 2, The HTTP Protocol*, presents the basics of the HTTP protocol and how it can be used in IoT applications. It also describes how it relates to the request/response and event subscription communication patterns.

*Chapter 3, The UPnP Protocol*, presents the basics of the UPnP protocol and how it can be used to discover devices in an ad hoc local area network. It also discusses how to call services on the devices and subscribe to events from them. Additionally, it describes how to build devices that publish such discoverable services and events.

*Chapter 4, The CoAP Protocol*, presents the basics of the CoAP protocol and how it can be used on devices that communicate over bandwidth-limited networks. It will show you how to publish content, how to subscribe to events, how to transport large content items using blocks, and how to discover existing resources on a device.

*Chapter 5, The MQTT Protocol*, introduces the MQTT protocol and shows how our IoT applications can bypass firewalls using the publish/subscribe communication pattern and message brokers.

*Chapter 6, The XMPP Protocol*, presents the XMPP protocol, and how it uses a federated set of message brokers to provide global identities and how it provides a richer set of communication patterns to the IoT developer. This chapter also introduces new communication patterns such as friendship authorization, presence subscription, asynchronous messaging, delegation of trust, and provisioning.

*Chapter 7, Using an IoT Service Platform*, presents reasons for using a service platform designed for IoT to facilitate rapid application development of IoT services and taking care of recurrent issues, such as security, interoperability, scalability, management, monitoring, and so on.

*Chapter 8, Creating Protocol Gateways*, shows you how to use good abstraction models to facilitate the creation of protocol bridges, allowing the interconnection of systems and services based on different technologies. This will enable you to design a secure and interoperable infrastructure for smart cities based on the IoT.

*Chapter 9, Security and Interoperability*, gives an overview of available threats and common modes of attack and how to build counter measures to protect your IoT solutions. It also shows the importance of interoperability in IoT and how to avoid limiting one to favor the other.

*Appendix A, Console Applications*, shows the basic structure of console applications, as used throughout the examples in this book.

*Appendix B, Sampling and History*, shows how sampling and historical record keeping of sensor values is done in the Sensor project published in this book.

*Appendix C, Object Database*, shows how to persist data in an object database, simply by using class definitions.

*Appendix D, Control*, shows how control operations are implemented in the Actuator project published in this book.

*Appendix E, Fundamentals of HTTP*, provides an overview of the fundamentals of the HTTP protocol.

*Appendix F, Sensor Data Query Parameters*, provides a set of query parameters we can use to limit readout requests from devices to data we are interested in.

*Appendix G, Security in HTTP*, discusses different ways to implement security into applications using the HTTP protocol.

*Appendix H, Delayed Responses in HTTP*, presents a method how to modify the request/response communication pattern used in HTTP to mimic the event subscription communication pattern.

*Appendix I, Fundamentals of UPnP*, provides an overview of the fundamentals of the UPnP protocol.

*Appendix J, Data Types in UPnP*, lists common data types used in UPnP.

# Preface

*Appendix K, Camera Web Interface*, presents a simple web interface publishing pictures taken by the camera.

*Appendix L, Text Encoding on the Web*, discusses text encoding on the web, and possible encoding conflicts.

*Appendix M, Sending Mail with Snapshots*, shows how to send mail including embedded snapshots taken by the camera.

*Appendix N, Tracking Cameras*, shows how the controller application tracks available cameras in the network.

*Appendix O, Certificates and Validation*, gives a short description of how certificates work, and how to install certificates on the Raspberry Pi.

*Appendix P, Chat Interfaces*, shows how to add a chat interface to your devices, making it possible to chat with them using standard chat applications based on XMPP.

*Appendix Q, QR Code*, shows a simple way to generate and display QR code.

*Appendix R, Bill of Materials*, contains bills of materials containing the components used for the boards used in the examples in this book.

These Appendices are not present in the book but are available for download at the following link: `https://www.packtpub.com/sites/default/files/downloads/3494_3532OT_Appendices.pdf`

# What you need for this book

Apart from a computer running Windows, Linux, or Mac OS, you will need four or five Raspberry Pi model B credit-card-sized computers, with SD cards containing the Raspbian operating system installed. *Appendix R, Bill of Materials*, which is available online, lists the components used to build the circuits used in the examples presented in the book.

The software used in this book is freely available on the Internet:

- A development environment for C#. This can be Xamarin, MonoDevelop, or VisualStudio. The first two are freely available, and the third has a free trial version that can be used.
    - Xamarin, available on Windows and Mac OS, can be downloaded from `http://xamarin.com/download`.

- ◦ MonoDevelop, for Linux (Debian, Ubuntu, Fedora, Red Hat, and openSUSE) can be downloaded from http://www.monodevelop.com/download/.
- ◦ A trial version of Visual Studio for Windows can be downloaded from http://www.visualstudio.com/downloads/download-visual-studio-vs.

- In *Chapter 4, The CoAP Protocol*, we will use the Copper (Cu) Firefox plugin to experiment with CoAP calls. It can be freely downloaded from https://addons.mozilla.org/en-US/firefox/addon/copper-270430/.

- For *Chapter 7, Using an IoT Service Platform*, and *Chapter 8, Creating Protocol Gateways*, we will use the Clayster IoT service platform called ClaysterSmall. Free licenses for private, test, or academic use, as well as the Clayster Management Tool, are available for download from http://www.clayster.com/downloads/.

- The source code for all the projects presented in this book is available for download from GitHub. See the section about downloading example code, which will follow, for details.

# Who this book is for

This book is for developers or electronics engineers who are curious about IoT. With only a rudimentary understanding of electronics (high-school level), Raspberry Pi or similar credit-card-sized computers, and some programming experience using managed code, such as C# or Java, or object-oriented language, such as C++, you will be taught to develop state-of-the-art solutions for the IoT in an instant.

# Conventions

In this book, you will find a number of styles of text that distinguish between different kinds of information. Here are some examples of these styles, and an explanation of their meaning.

Code words in text, database table names, folder names, filenames, file extensions, pathnames, dummy URLs, user input, and Twitter handles are shown as follows: "For instance, Digital outputs are handled using the DigitalOutput class."

A block of code is set as follows:

```
private static DigitalOutput executionLed =
  new DigitalOutput (23, true);
private static DigitalOutput measurementLed =
  new DigitalOutput (24, false);
private static DigitalOutput errorLed =
  new DigitalOutput (25, false);
private static DigitalOutput networkLed =
  new DigitalOutput (18, false);
```

Any command-line input or output is written as follows:

```
$ sudo apt-get udpate
$ sudo apt-get upgrade
$ sudo apt-get install mono-complete
```

New terms and important words such as "**Internet of Things (IoT)**" are shown in bold. Words that you see on the screen, in menus or dialog boxes for example, appear in the text like this: "To be able to configure the screen as we want, we enter the **Settings** menu, click on the **Layout** menu item, and select the **No Menu 5x4** option ".

> Warnings or important notes appear in a box like this.

> Tips and tricks appear like this.

# Reader feedback

Feedback from our readers is always welcome. Let us know what you think about this book—what you liked or may have disliked. Reader feedback is important for us to develop titles that you really get the most out of.

To send us general feedback, simply send an e-mail to feedback@packtpub.com, and mention the book title via the subject of your message.

If there is a topic that you have expertise in and you are interested in either writing or contributing to a book, see our author guide on www.packtpub.com/authors.

# Customer support

Now that you are the proud owner of a Packt book, we have a number of things to help you to get the most from your purchase.

# Downloading the example code

The code for the example projects presented in this book, are available for download from GitHub. The following table shows where each solution is published:

| Chapter | Project name | URL |
| --- | --- | --- |
| 1-2 | Learning-IoT-HTTP | https://github.com/Clayster/Learning-IoT-HTTP |
| 3 | Learning-IoT-UPnP | https://github.com/Clayster/Learning-IoT-UPnP |
| 4 | Learning-IoT-CoAP | https://github.com/Clayster/Learning-IoT-CoAP |
| 5 | Learning-IoT-MQTT | https://github.com/Clayster/Learning-IoT-MQTT |
| 6 | Learning-IoT-XMPP | https://github.com/Clayster/Learning-IoT-XMPP |
| 7 | Learning-IoT-IoTPlatform | https://github.com/Clayster/Learning-IoT-IoTPlatform |
| 8 | Learning-IoT-Gateway | https://github.com/Clayster/Learning-IoT-Gateway |

# Viewing or downloading the online appendices

You can view or download appendices A to R for this Packt book from your account at http://www.packtpub.com. If you purchased this book elsewhere, you can visit https://www.packtpub.com/books/content/support and register to have the files e-mailed directly to you. Note that a URL is mentioned above, to download the appendices:

https://www.packtpub.com/sites/default/files/downloads/3494_3532OT_Appendices.pdf

# Errata

Although we have taken every care to ensure the accuracy of our content, mistakes do happen. If you find a mistake in one of our books—maybe a mistake in the text or the code—we would be grateful if you would report this to us. By doing so, you can save other readers from frustration and help us improve subsequent versions of this book. If you find any errata, please report them by visiting http://www.packtpub.com/submit-errata, selecting your book, clicking on the **errata submission form** link, and entering the details of your errata. Once your errata are verified, your submission will be accepted and the errata will be uploaded on our website, or added to any list of existing errata, under the Errata section of that title. Any existing errata can be viewed by selecting your title from http://www.packtpub.com/support.

# Piracy

Piracy of copyright material on the Internet is an ongoing problem across all media. At Packt, we take the protection of our copyright and licenses very seriously. If you come across any illegal copies of our works, in any form, on the Internet, please provide us with the location address or website name immediately so that we can pursue a remedy.

Please contact us at copyright@packtpub.com with a link to the suspected pirated material.

We appreciate your help in protecting our authors, and our ability to bring you valuable content.

# Questions

You can contact us at questions@packtpub.com if you are having a problem with any aspect of the book, and we will do our best to address it.

# 1
# Preparing our IoT Projects

This book will cover a series of projects for Raspberry Pi that cover very common and handy use cases within **Internet of Things (IoT)**. These projects include the following:

- **Sensor**: This project is used to sense physical values and publish them together with metadata on the Internet in various ways.
- **Actuator**: This performs actions in the physical world based on commands it receives from the Internet.
- **Controller**: This is a device that provides application intelligence to the Internet.
- **Camera**: This is a device that publishes a camera through which you will take pictures.
- **Bridge**: This is the fifth and final project, which is a device that acts as a bridge between different protocols. We will cover this at an introductory level later in the book (*Chapter 8, Creating Protocol Gateways*, if you would like to take a look at it now), as it relies on the IoT service platform.

Before delving into the different protocols used in Internet of Things, we will dedicate some time in this chapter to set up some of these projects, present circuit diagrams, and perform basic measurement and control operations, which are not specific to any communication protocol. The following chapters will then use this code as the basis for the new code presented in each chapter.

> All of the source code presented in this book is available for download. The source code for this chapter and the next one can be downloaded from `https://github.com/Clayster/Learning-IoT-HTTP`.

*Preparing our IoT Projects*

Along with the project preparation phase, you will also learn about some of the following concepts in this chapter:

- Development using C# for Raspberry Pi
- The basic project structure
- Introduction to Clayster libraries
- The sensor, actuator, controller, and camera projects
- Interfacing the General Purpose Input/Output pins
- Circuit diagrams
- Hardware interfaces
- Introduction to interoperability in IoT
- Data persistence using an object database

# Creating the sensor project

Our first project will be the sensor project. Since it is the first one, we will cover it in more detail than the following projects in this book. A majority of what we will explore will also be reutilized in other projects as much as possible. The development of the sensor is broken down into six steps, and the source code for each step can be downloaded separately. You will find a simple overview of this here:

1. Firstly, you will set up the basic structure of a console application.
2. Then, you will configure the hardware and learn to sample sensor values and maintain a useful historical record.
3. After adding HTTP server capabilities as well as useful web resources to the project, you will publish the sensor values collected on the Internet.
4. You will then handle persistence of sampled data in the sensor so it can resume after outages or software updates.
5. The next step will teach you how to add a security layer, requiring user authentication to access sensitive information, on top of the application.
6. In the last step, you will learn how to overcome one of the major obstacles in the request/response pattern used by HTTP, that is, how to send events from the server to the client.

> Only the first two steps are presented here, and the rest in the following chapter, since they introduce HTTP. The fourth step will be introduced in this chapter but will be discussed in more detail in *Appendix C, Object Database*.

[ 12 ]

# Preparing Raspberry Pi

I assume that you are familiar with Raspberry Pi and have it configured. If not, refer to http://www.raspberrypi.org/help/faqs/#buyingWhere.

In our examples, we will use Model B with the following:

- An SD card with the Raspbian operating system installed
- A configured network access, including Wi-Fi, if used
- User accounts, passwords, access rights, time zones, and so on, all configured correctly

 I also assume that you know how to create and maintain terminal connections with the device and transfer files to and from the device.

All our examples will be developed on a remote PC (for instance, a normal working laptop) using C# (C + + + + if you like to think of it this way), as this is a modern programming language that allows us to do what we want to do with IoT. It also allows us to interchange code between Windows, Linux, Macintosh, Android, and iOS platforms.

 Don't worry about using C#. Developers with knowledge in C, C++, or Java should have no problems understanding it.

Once a project is compiled, executable files are deployed to the corresponding Raspberry Pi (or Raspberry Pi boards) and then executed. Since the code runs on .NET, any language out of the large number of CLI-compatible languages can be used.

 Development tools for C# can be downloaded for free from http://xamarin.com/.

To prepare Raspberry for the execution of the .NET code, we need to install Mono, which contains the Common Language Runtime for .NET that will help us run the .NET code on Raspberry. This is done by executing the following commands in a terminal window in Raspberry Pi:

```
$ sudo apt-get update
$ sudo apt-get upgrade
$ sudo apt-get install mono-complete
```

Your device is now ready to run the .NET code.

# Clayster libraries

To facilitate the development of IoT applications, this book provides you with the right to use seven Clayster libraries for private and commercial applications. These are available on GitHub with the downloadable source code for each chapter. Of these seven libraries, two are provided with the source code so that the community can extend them as they desire. Furthermore, the source code of all the examples shown in this book is also available for download.

The following Clayster libraries are included:

| Library | Description |
| --- | --- |
| `Clayster.Library.Data` | This provides the application with a powerful object database. Objects are persisted and can be searched directly in the code using the object's class definition. No database coding is necessary. Data can be stored in the SQLite database provided in Raspberry Pi. |
| `Clayster.Library.EventLog` | This provides the application with an extensible event logging architecture that can be used to get an overview of what happens in a network of things. |
| `Clayster.Library.Internet` | This contains classes that implement common Internet protocols. Applications can use these to communicate over the Internet in a dynamic manner. |
| `Clayster.Library.Language` | This provides mechanisms to create localizable applications that are simple to translate and that can work in an international setting. |
| `Clayster.Library.Math` | This provides a powerful extensible, mathematical scripting language that can help with automation, scripting, graph plotting, and others. |
| `Clayster.Library.IoT` | This provides classes that help applications become interoperable by providing data representation and parsing capabilities of data in IoT. The source code is also included here. |
| `Clayster.Library.RaspberryPi` | This contains **Hardware Abstraction Layer (HAL)** for Raspberry Pi. It provides object-oriented interfaces to interact with devices connected to the **General Purpose Input/Output (GPIO)** pins available. The source code is also included here. |

# Hardware

Our sensor prototype will measure three things: light, temperature, and motion. To summarize, here is a brief description of the components:

- The light sensor is a simple ZX-LDR analog sensor that we will connect to a four-channel (of which we use only one) analog-to-digital converter (Digilent Pmod AD2), which is connected to an I²C bus that we will connect to the standard GPIO pins for I²C.

>
> The I²C bus permits communication with multiple circuits using synchronous communication that employs a **Serial Clock Line** (**SCL**) and **Serial Data Line** (**SDA**) pin. This is a common way to communicate with integrated circuits.

- The temperature sensor (Texas Instruments TMP102) connects directly to the same I²C bus.
- The SCL and SDA pins on the I²C bus use recommended pull-up resistors to make sure they are in a high state when nobody actively pulls them down.
- The infrared motion detector (Parallax PIR sensor) is a digital input that we connect to GPIO 22.
- We also add four LEDs to the board. One of these is green and is connected to GPIO 23. This will show when the application is running. The second one is yellow and is connected to GPIO 24. This will show when measurements are done. The third one is yellow and is connected to GPIO 18. This will show when an HTTP activity is performed. The last one is red and is connected to GPIO 25. This will show when a communication error occurs.
- The pins that control the LEDs are first connected to 160 Ω resistors before they are connected to the LEDs, and then to ground. All the hardware of the prototype board is powered by the 3.3 V source provided by Raspberry Pi. A 160 Ω resistor connected in series between the pin and ground makes sure 20 mA flows through the LED, which makes it emit a bright light.

>
> For an introduction to GPIO on Raspberry Pi, please refer to `http://www.raspberrypi.org/documentation/usage/gpio/`.
> Two guides on GPIO pins can be found at `http://elinux.org/RPi_Low-level_peripherals`.
> For more information, refer to `http://pi.gadgetoid.com/pinout`.

*Preparing our IoT Projects*

The following figure shows a circuit diagram of our prototype board:

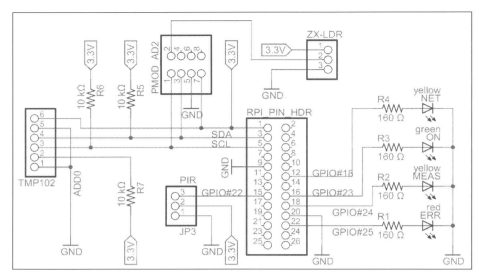

A circuit diagram for the Sensor project

For a bill of materials containing the components used, see *Appendix R, Bill of Materials*.

# Interacting with our hardware

We also need to create a console application project in Xamarin. *Appendix A, Console Applications*, details how to set up a console application in Xamarin and how to enable event logging and then compile, deploy, and execute the code on Raspberry Pi.

Interaction with our hardware is done using corresponding classes defined in the `Clayster.Library.RaspberryPi` library, for which the source code is provided. For instance, digital output is handled using the `DigitalOutput` class and digital input with the `DigitalInput` class. Devices connected to an I²C bus are handled using the `I2C` class. There are also other generic classes, such as `ParallelDigitalInput` and `ParallelDigitalOutput`, that handle a series of digital input and output at once. The `SoftwarePwm` class handles a software-controlled pulse-width modulation output. The `Uart` class handles communication using the UART port available on Raspberry Pi. There's also a subnamespace called `Devices` where device-specific classes are available.

In the end, all classes communicate with the static GPIO class, which is used to interact with the GPIO layer in Raspberry Pi.

Each class has a constructor that initializes the corresponding hardware resource, methods and properties to interact with the resource, and finally a Dispose method that releases the resource.

It is very important that you release the hardware resources allocated before you terminate the application. Since hardware resources are not controlled by the operating system, the fact that the application is terminated is not sufficient to release the resources. For this reason, make sure you call the Dispose methods of all the allocated hardware resources before you leave the application. Preferably, this should be done in the finally statement of a try-finally block.

## Interfacing the hardware

The hardware interfaces used for our LEDs are as follows:

```
private static DigitalOutput executionLed =
   new DigitalOutput (23, true);
private static DigitalOutput measurementLed =
   new DigitalOutput (24, false);
private static DigitalOutput errorLed =
   new DigitalOutput (25, false);
private static DigitalOutput networkLed =
   new DigitalOutput (18, false);
```

We use a DigitalInput class for our motion detector:

```
private static DigitalInput motion = new DigitalInput (22);
```

With our temperature sensor on the I²C bus, which limits the serial clock frequency to a maximum of 400 kHz, we interface as follows:

```
private static I2C i2cBus = new I2C (3, 2, 400000);
private static TexasInstrumentsTMP102 tmp102 =
   new TexasInstrumentsTMP102 (0, i2cBus);
```

We interact with the light sensor using an analog-to-digital converter as follows:

```
private static AD799x adc =
   new AD799x (0, true, false, false, false, i2cBus);
```

## Internal representation of sensor values

The sensor data values will be represented by the following set of variables:

```
private static bool motionDetected = false;
private static double temperatureC;
private static double lightPercent;
private static object synchObject = new object ();
```

Historical values will also be kept so that trends can be analyzed:

```
private static List<Record> perSecond = new List<Record> ();
private static List<Record> perMinute = new List<Record> ();
private static List<Record> perHour = new List<Record> ();
private static List<Record> perDay = new List<Record> ();
private static List<Record> perMonth = new List<Record> ();
```

>  *Appendix B, Sampling and History*, describes how to perform basic sensor value sampling and historical record keeping in more detail using the hardware interfaces defined earlier. It also describes the `Record` class.

## Persisting data

Persisting data is simple. This is done using an **object database**. This object database analyzes the class definition of objects to persist and dynamically creates the database schema to accommodate the objects you want to store. The object database is defined in the `Clayster.Library.Data` library. You first need a reference to the object database, which is as follows:

```
internal static ObjectDatabase db;
```

Then, you need to provide information on how to connect to the underlying database. This can be done in the `.config` file of the application or the code itself. In our case, we will specify a SQLite database and provide the necessary parameters in the code during the startup:

```
DB.BackupConnectionString = "Data Source=sensor.db;Version=3;";
DB.BackupProviderName = "Clayster.Library.Data.Providers." +
  "SQLiteServer.SQLiteServerProvider";
```

Finally, you will get a proxy object for the object database as follows. This object can be used to store, update, delete, and search for objects in your database:

```
db = DB.GetDatabaseProxy ("TheSensor");
```

>  *Appendix C, Object Database*, shows how the data collected in this application is persisted using only the available class definitions through the use of this object database.

By doing this, the sensor does not lose data if Raspberry Pi is restarted.

# External representation of sensor values

To facilitate the interchange of sensor data between devices, an interoperable sensor data format based on XML is provided in the `Clayster.Library.IoT` library. There, sensor data consists of a collection of nodes that report data ordered according to the timestamp. For each timestamp, a collection of fields is reported. There are different types of fields available: numerical, string, date and time, timespan, Boolean, and enumeration-valued fields. Each field has a field name, field value of the corresponding type and the optional readout type (if the value corresponds to a momentary value, peak value, status value, and so on), a field status, or Quality of Service value and localization information.

The `Clayster.Library.IoT.SensorData` namespace helps us export sensor data information by providing an abstract interface called `ISensorDataExport`. The same logic can later be used to export to different sensor data formats. The library also provides a class named `ReadoutRequest` that provides information about what type of data is desired. We can use this to tailor the data export to the desires of the requestor.

# Exporting sensor data

The export starts by calling the `Start()` method on the sensor data export module and ends with a call to the `End()` method. Between these two, a sequence of `StartNode()` and `EndNode()` method calls are made, one for each node to export. To simplify our export, we then call another function to output data from an array of `Record` objects that contain our data. We use the same method to export our momentary values by creating a temporary `Record` object that would contain them:

```
private static void ExportSensorData (ISensorDataExport Output,
  ReadoutRequest Request)
{
  Output.Start ();
  lock (synchObject)
  {
    Output.StartNode ("Sensor");
```

*Preparing our IoT Projects*

```
      Export (Output, new Record[]
        {
          new Record (DateTime.Now, temperatureC, lightPercent,
            motionDetected)
        },ReadoutType.MomentaryValues, Request);
      Export (Output, perSecond, ReadoutType.HistoricalValuesSecond,
        Request);
      Export (Output, perMinute, ReadoutType.HistoricalValuesMinute,
        Request);
      Export (Output, perHour, ReadoutType.HistoricalValuesHour,
        Request);
      Export (Output, perDay, ReadoutType.HistoricalValuesDay,
        Request);
      Export (Output, perMonth, ReadoutType.HistoricalValuesMonth,
        Request);
      Output.EndNode ();
    }
    Output.End ();
}
```

For each array of `Record` objects, we then export them as follows:

 It is important to note here that we need to check whether the corresponding readout type is desired by the client before you export data of this type.

The `Export` method exports an enumeration of `Record` objects as follows. First it checks whether the corresponding readout type is desired by the client before exporting data of this type. The method also checks whether the data is within any time interval requested and that the fields are of interest to the client. If a data field passes all these tests, it is exported by calling any of the instances of the overloaded method `ExportField()`, available on the sensor data export object. Fields are exported between the `StartTimestamp()` and `EndTimestamp()` method calls, defining the timestamp that corresponds to the fields being exported:

```
private static void Export(ISensorDataExport Output,
  IEnumerable<Record> History, ReadoutType Type,
  ReadoutRequest Request)
{
  if((Request.Types & Type) != 0)
  {
    foreach(Record Rec in History)
    {
      if(!Request.ReportTimestamp (Rec.Timestamp))
```

```
        continue;

      Output.StartTimestamp(Rec.Timestamp);

    if (Request.ReportField("Temperature"))
      Output.ExportField("Temperature",Rec.TemperatureC,
        1,"C", Type);

    if(Request.ReportField("Light"))
      Output.ExportField("Light",Rec.LightPercent, 1, "%",
        Type);

    if(Request.ReportField ("Motion"))
      Output.ExportField("Motion",Rec.Motion, Type);

      Output.EndTimestamp();
    }
  }
}
```

We can test the method by exporting some sensor data to XML using the `SensorDataXmlExport` class. It implements the `ISensorDataExport` interface. The result would look something like this if you export only momentary and historic day values.

 The ellipsis (...) represents a sequence of historical day records, similar to the one that precedes it, and newline and indentation has been inserted for readability.

```
<?xml version="1.0"?>
<fields xmlns="urn:xmpp:iot:sensordata">
  <node nodeId="Sensor">
    <timestamp value="2014-07-25T12:29:32Z">
      <numeric value="19.2" unit="C" automaticReadout="true"
        momentary="true" name="Temperature"/>
      <numeric value="48.5" unit="%" automaticReadout="true"
        momentary="true" name="Light"/>
      <boolean value="true" automaticReadout="true"
        momentary="true" name="Motion"/>
    </timestamp>
    <timestamp value="2014-07-25T04:00:00Z">
      <numeric value="20.6" unit="C" automaticReadout="true"
        name="Temperature" historicalDay="true"/>
```

```
            <numeric value="13.0" unit="%" automaticReadout="true"
              name="Light" historicalDay="true"/>
            <boolean value="true" automaticReadout="true" name="Motion"
              historicalDay="true"/>
        </timestamp>
  ...
    </node>
</fields>
```

# Creating the actuator project

Another very common type of object used in automation and IoT is the actuator. While the sensor is used to sense physical magnitudes or events, an actuator is used to control events or act with the physical world. We will create a simple actuator that can be run on a standalone Raspberry Pi. This actuator will have eight digital outputs and one alarm output. The actuator will not have any control logic in it by itself. Instead, interfaces will be published, thereby making it possible for controllers to use the actuator for their own purposes.

> In the sensor project, we went through the details on how to create an IoT application based on HTTP. In this project, we will reuse much of what has already been done and not explicitly go through these steps again. We will only list what is different.

## Hardware

Our actuator prototype will control eight digital outputs and one alarm output:

- Each one of the digital output is connected to a 160 Ω resistor and a red LED to ground. If the output is high, the LED is turned on. We have connected the LEDs to the GPIO pins in this order: 18, 4, 17, 27, 22, 25, 24, and 23. If Raspberry Pi R1 is used, GPIO pin 27 should be renumbered to 21.

- For the alarm output, we connect a speaker to GPIO pin 7 (CE1) and then to ground. We also add a connection from GPIO 8 (CE0), a 160 Ω resistor to a green LED, and then to ground. The green LED will show when the application is being executed.

> For a bill of materials containing components used, refer to *Appendix R, Bill of Materials*.

The actuator project can be better understood with the following circuit diagram:

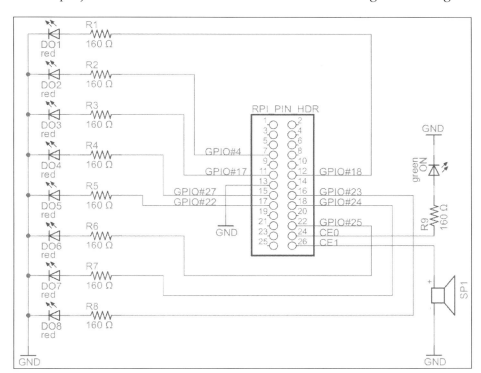

A circuit diagram for the actuator project

## Interfacing the hardware

All the hardware interfaces except the alarm output are simple digital outputs. They can be controlled by the `DigitalOutput` class. The alarm output will control the speaker through a square wave signal that will be output on GPIO pin 7 using the `SoftwarePwm` class, which outputs a pulse-width-modulated square signal on one or more digital outputs. The `SoftwarePwm` class will only be created when the output is active. When not active, the pin will be left as a digital input.

The declarations look as follows:

```
private static DigitalOutput executionLed =
new DigitalOutput (8, true);
private static SoftwarePwm alarmOutput = null;
private static Thread alarmThread = null;
private static DigitalOutput[] digitalOutputs =
   new DigitalOutput[]
```

```
{
    new DigitalOutput (18, false),
    new DigitalOutput (4, false),
    new DigitalOutput (17, false),
    new DigitalOutput (27, false),// pin 21 on RaspberryPi R1
    new DigitalOutput (22, false),
    new DigitalOutput (25, false),
    new DigitalOutput (24, false),
    new DigitalOutput (23, false)
};
```

Digital output is controlled using the objects in the `digitalOutputs` array directly. The alarm is controlled by calling the `AlarmOn()` and `AlarmOff()` methods.

> *Appendix D, Control*, details how these hardware interfaces are used to perform control operations.

## Creating a controller

We have a sensor that provides sensing and an actuator that provides actuating. But none have any intelligence yet. The controller application provides intelligence to the network. It will consume data from the sensor, then draw logical conclusions and use the actuator to inform the world of its conclusions.

The controller we create will read the ambient light and motion detection provided by the sensor. If it is dark and there exists movement, the controller will sound the alarm. The controller will also use the LEDs of the controller to display how much light is being reported.

> Of the three applications we have presented thus far, this application is the simplest to implement since it does not publish any information that needs to be protected. Instead, it uses two other applications through the interfaces they have published. The project does not use any particular hardware either.

# Representing sensor values

The first step toward creating a controller is to access sensors from where relevant data can be retrieved. We will duplicate sensor data into these private member variables:

```
private static bool motion = false;
private static double lightPercent = 0;
private static bool hasValues = false;
```

In the following chapter, we will show you different methods to populate these variables with values by using different communication protocols. Here, we will simply assume the variables have been populated by the correct sensor values.

# Parsing sensor data

We get help from `Clayster.Library.IoT.SensorData` to parse data in XML format, generated by the sensor data export we discussed earlier. So, all we need to do is loop through the fields that are received and extract the relevant information as follows. We return a Boolean value that would indicate whether the field values read were different from the previous ones:

```
private static bool UpdateFields(XmlDocument Xml)
{
  FieldBoolean Boolean;
  FieldNumeric Numeric;
  bool Updated = false;

  foreach (Field F in Import.Parse(Xml))
  {
    if(F.FieldName == "Motion" &&
      (Boolean = F as FieldBoolean) != null)
    {
      if(!hasValues || motion != Boolean.Value)
      {
        motion = Boolean.Value;
        Updated = true;
      }
    } else if(F.FieldName == "Light" &&
      (Numeric = F as FieldNumeric) != null &&
      Numeric.Unit == "%")
    {
      if(!hasValues || lightPercent != Numeric.Value)
      {
        lightPercent = Numeric.Value;
```

```
            Updated = true;
        }
      }
    }

    return Updated;
}
```

## Calculating control states

The controller needs to calculate which LEDs to light along with the state of the alarm output based on the values received by the sensor. The controlling of the actuator can be done from a separate thread so that communication with the actuator does not affect the communication with the sensor, and the other way around. Communication between the main thread that is interacting with the sensor and the control thread is done using two `AutoResetEvent` objects and a couple of control state variables:

```
private static AutoResetEvent updateLeds =
   new AutoResetEvent(false);
private static AutoResetEvent updateAlarm =
   new AutoResetEvent(false);
private static int lastLedMask = -1;
private static bool? lastAlarm = null;
private static object synchObject = new object();
```

We have eight LEDs to control. We will turn them off if the sensor reports 0 percent light and light them all if the sensor reports 100 percent light. The control action we will use takes a byte where each LED is represented by a bit. The alarm is to be sounded when there is less than 20 percent light reported and the motion is detected. The calculations are done as follows:

```
private static void CheckControlRules()
{
   int NrLeds = (int)System.Math.Round((8 * lightPercent) / 100);
   int LedMask = 0;
   int i = 1;
   bool Alarm;

   while(NrLeds > 0)
   {
      NrLeds--;
      LedMask |= i;
      i <<= 1;
```

```
        }

        Alarm = lightPercent < 20 && motion;
```

We then compare these results with the previous ones to see whether we need to inform the control thread to send control commands:

```
        lock(synchObject)
        {
          if(LedMask != lastLedMask)
          {
            lastLedMask = LedMask;
            updateLeds.Set();
          }

          if (!lastAlarm.HasValue || lastAlarm.Value != Alarm)
          {
            lastAlarm = Alarm;
            updateAlarm.Set();
          }
        }
    }
```

## Creating a camera

In this book, we will also introduce a camera project. This device will use an infrared camera that will be published in the network, and it will be used by the controller to take pictures when the alarm goes off.

## Hardware

For our camera project, we've chosen to use the LinkSprite JPEG infrared color camera instead of the normal Raspberry Camera module or a normal UVC camera. It allows us to take photos during the night and leaves us with two USB slots free for Wi-Fi and keyboard. You can take a look at the essential information about the camera by visiting http://www.linksprite.com/upload/file/1291522825.pdf. Here is a summary of the circuit connections:

- The camera has a serial interface that we can use through the UART available on Raspberry Pi. It has four pins, two of which are reception pin (**RX**) and transmission pin (**TX**) and the other two are connected to 5 V and ground **GND** respectively.

- The **RX** and **TX** on the Raspberry Pi pin header are connected to the **TX** and **RX** on the camera, respectively. In parallel, we connect the **TX** and **RX** lines to a logical inverter. Then, via 240 Ω resistors, we connect them to two LEDs, yellow for **TX** and green for **RX**, and then to **GND**. Since **TX** and **RX** are normally high and are drawn low during communication, we need to invert the signals so that the LEDs remain unlit when there is no communication and they blink when communication is happening.
- We also connect four GPIO pins (18, 23, 24, and 25) via 160 Ω resistors to four LEDs and ground to signal the different states in our application. GPIO 18 controls a green LED signal when the camera application is running. GPIO 23 and 24 control yellow LEDs; the first GPIO controls the LED when communication with the camera is being performed, and the second controls the LED when a network request is being handled. GPIO 25 controls a red LED, and it is used to show whether an error has occurred somewhere.

This project can be better understood with the following circuit diagram:

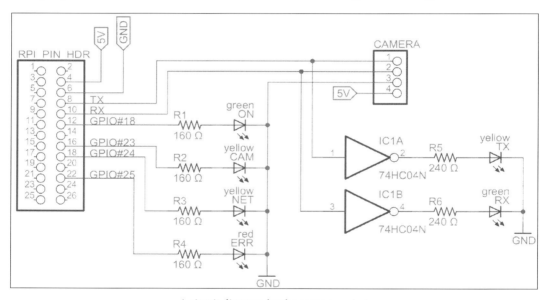

A circuit diagram for the camera project

 For a bill of materials containing components used, see *Appendix R, Bill of Materials*.

# Accessing the serial port on Raspberry Pi

To be able to access the serial port on Raspberry Pi from the code, we must first make sure that the Linux operating system does not use it for other purposes. The serial port is called `ttyAMA0` in the operating system, and we need to remove references to it from two operating system files: `/boot/cmdline.txt` and `/etc/inittab`. This will disable access to the Raspberry Pi console via the serial port. But we will still be able to access it using SSH or a USB keyboard. From a command prompt, you can edit the first file as follows:

```
$ sudo nano /boot/cmdline.txt
```

You need to edit the second file as well, as follows:

```
$ sudo nano /etc/inittab
```

> For more detailed information, refer to the `http://elinux.org/RPi_Serial_Connection#Preventing_Linux_using_the_serial_port` article and read the section on how to prevent Linux from using the serial port.

# Interfacing the hardware

To interface the hardware laid out on our prototype board, we will use the `Clayster.Library.RaspberryPi` library. We control the LEDs using `DigitalOutput` objects:

```
private static DigitalOutput executionLed =
   new DigitalOutput (18, true);
private static DigitalOutput cameraLed =
   new DigitalOutput (23, false);
private static DigitalOutput networkLed =
   new DigitalOutput (24, false);
private static DigitalOutput errorLed =
   new DigitalOutput (25, false);
```

The LinkSprite camera is controlled by the `LinkSpriteJpegColorCamera` class in the `Clayster.Library.RaspberryPi.Devices.Cameras` subnamespace. It uses the `Uart` class to perform serial communication. Both these classes are available in the downloadable source code:

```
private static LinkSpriteJpegColorCamera camera =
   new LinkSpriteJpegColorCamera
   (LinkSpriteJpegColorCamera.BaudRate.Baud__38400);
```

## Creating persistent default settings

For our camera to work, we need four persistent and configurable default settings: camera resolution, compression level, image encoding, and an identity for our device. To achieve this, we create a `DefaultSettings` class that we can persist in the object database:

```
public class DefaultSettings : DBObject
{
  private LinkSpriteJpegColorCamera.ImageSize resolution =
    LinkSpriteJpegColorCamera.ImageSize._320x240;
  private byte compressionLevel = 0x36;
  private string imageEncoding = "image/jpeg";
  private string udn = Guid.NewGuid().ToString();

  public DefaultSettings() : base(MainClass.db)
  {
  }
}
```

## Adding configurable properties

We publish the camera `resolution` property as follows. The three possible enumeration values are: `ImageSize_160x120`, `ImageSize_320x240`, and `ImageSize_640x480`. These correspond to the three different resolutions supported by the camera:

```
[DBDefault (LinkSpriteJpegColorCamera.ImageSize._320x240)]
public LinkSpriteJpegColorCamera.ImageSize Resolution
{
  get
  {
    return this.resolution;
  }
  set
  {
    if (this.resolution != value)
    {
      this.resolution = value;
      this.Modified = true;
    }
  }
}
```

We publish the compression-level property in a similar manner.

Internally, the camera only supports JPEG-encoding of the pictures that are taken. But in our project, we will add software support for PNG and BMP compression as well. To make things simple and extensible, we choose to store the image-encoding method as a string containing the Internet media type of the encoding scheme implied:

```
[DBShortStringClipped (false)]
[DBDefault ("image/jpeg")]
public string ImageEncoding
{
  get
  {
    return this.imageEncoding;
  }
  set
  {
    if(this.imageEncoding != value)
    {
      this.imageEncoding = value;
      this.Modified = true;
    }
  }
}
```

## Persisting the settings

We add a method to load any persisted settings from the object database:

```
    public static DefaultSettings LoadSettings()
    {
      return MainClass.db.FindObjects
        <DefaultSettings>().GetEarliestCreatedDeleteOthers();
    }
}
```

In our main application, we create a variable to hold our default settings. We make sure to define it as internal using the `internal` access specifier so that we can access it from other classes in our project:

```
    internal static DefaultSettings defaultSettings;
```

During application initialization, we load any default settings available from previous executions of the application. If none are found, the default settings are created and initiated to the default values of the corresponding properties, including a new GUID identifying the device instance in the UDN property the UDN property:

```
    defaultSettings = DefaultSettings.LoadSettings();
    if(defaultSettings == null)
```

```
{
  defaultSettings = new DefaultSettings();
  defaultSettings.SaveNew();
}
```

## Working with the current settings

To avoid having to reconfigure the camera every time a picture is to be taken, something that is time-consuming, we need to remember what the current settings are and avoid reconfiguring the camera unless new properties are used. These current settings do not need to be persisted since we can reinitialize the camera every time the application is restarted. We declare our current settings parameters as follows:

```
private static LinkSpriteJpegColorCamera.ImageSize
    currentResolution;
private static byte currentCompressionRatio;
```

## Initializing the camera

During application initialization, we need to initialize the camera. First, we get the default settings as follows:

```
Log.Information("Initializing camera.");
try
{
  currentResolution = defaultSettings.Resolution;
  currentCompressionRatio = defaultSettings.CompressionLevel;
```

Here, we need to reset the camera and set the default image resolution. After changing the resolution, a new reset of the camera is required. All of this is done on the camera's default baud rate, which is 38,400 baud:

```
try
{
  camera.Reset();// First try @ 38400 baud
  camera.SetImageSize(currentResolution);
  camera.Reset();
```

Since image transfer is slow, we then try to set the highest baud rate supported by the camera:

```
camera.SetBaudRate
    (LinkSpriteJpegColorCamera.BaudRate.Baud_115200);
camera.Dispose();
camera = new LinkSpriteJpegColorCamera
    (LinkSpriteJpegColorCamera.BaudRate.Baud_115200);
```

If the preceding procedure fails, an exception will be thrown. The most probable cause for this to fail, if the hardware is working correctly, is that the application has been restarted and the camera is already working at 115,200 baud. This will be the case during development, for instance. In this case, we simply set the camera to 115,200 baud and continue. Here is room for improved error handling, and trying out different options to recover from more complex error conditions and synchronize the current states with the states of the camera:

```
}
catch(Exception) // If already at 115200 baud.
{
  camera.Dispose ();
  camera = new LinkSpriteJpegColorCamera
    (LinkSpriteJpegColorCamera.BaudRate.Baud_115200);
```

We then set the camera compression rate as follows:

```
}finally
{
  camera.SetCompressionRatio(currentCompressionRatio);
}
```

If this fails, we log the error to the event log and light our error LED to inform the end user that there is a failure:

```
}catch(Exception ex)
{
  Log.Exception(ex);
  errorLed.High();
  camera = null;
}
```

# Summary

In this chapter, we presented most of the projects that will be discussed in this book, together with circuit diagrams that show how to connect our hardware components. We also introduced development using C# for Raspberry Pi and presented the basic project structure. Several Clayster libraries were also introduced that help us with common programming tasks such as communication, interoperability, scripting, event logging, interfacing GPIO, and data persistence.

In the next chapter, we will introduce our first communication protocol for the IoT: The Hypertext Transfer Protocol (HTTP).

# 2
# The HTTP Protocol

Now that we have a definition for Internet of Things, where do we start? It is safe to assume that most people that use a computer today have had an experience of **Hypertext Transfer Protocol (HTTP)**, perhaps without even knowing it. When they "surf the Web", what they do is they navigate between pages using a browser that communicates with the server using HTTP. Some even go so far as identifying the Internet with the Web when they say they "go on the Internet" or "search the Internet".

Yet HTTP has become much more than navigation between pages on the Internet. Today, it is also used in **machine to machine** (**M2M**) communication, automation, and Internet of Things, among other things. So much is done on the Internet today, using the HTTP protocol, because it is easily accessible and easy to relate to. For this reason, we are starting our study of Internet of Things by studying HTTP. This will allow you to get a good grasp of its strengths and weaknesses, even though it is perhaps one of the more technically complex protocols. We will present the basic features of HTTP; look at the different available HTTP methods; study the request/response pattern and the ways to handle events, user authentication, and web services.

Before we begin, let's review some of the basic concepts used in HTTP which we will be looking at:

- The basics of HTTP
- How to add HTTP support to the sensor, actuator, and controller projects
- How common communication patterns such as request/response and event subscription can be utilized using HTTP

# HTTP basics

HTTP is a stateless request/response protocol where clients request information from a server and the server responds to these requests accordingly. A request is basically made up of a method, a resource, some headers, and some optional content. A response is made up of a three-digit status code, some headers and some optional content. This can be observed in the following diagram:

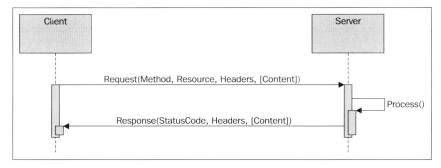

HTTP request/response pattern

Each resource, originally thought to be a collection of Hypertext documents or HTML documents, is identified by a **Uniform Resource Locator (URL)**. Clients simply use the GET method to request a resource from the corresponding server. In the structure of the URL presented next, the resource is identified by the path and the server by the authority portions of the URL. The PUT and DELETE methods allow clients to upload and remove content from the server, while the POST method allows them to send data to a resource on the server, for instance, in a web form. The structure of a URL is shown in the following diagram:

$$\underbrace{http}_{scheme} :// \underbrace{\overbrace{example.com}^{domain} : \overbrace{8080}^{port}}_{authority} \underbrace{/d/1.htm}_{path} ? \underbrace{q1=v1}_{query} \# \underbrace{f0011}_{fragment}$$

Structure of a Uniform Resource Locator (URL)

HTTP defines a set of headers that can be used to attach metainformation about the requests and responses sent over the network. These headers are human readable key - value text pairs that contain information about how content is encoded, for how long it is valid, what type of content is desired, and so on. The type of content is identified by a **Content-Type** header, which identifies the type of content that is being transmitted. Headers also provide a means to authenticate clients to the server and a mechanism to introduce states in HTTP. By introducing cookies, which are text strings, the servers can ask the client to remember the cookies, which the client can then add to each request that is made to the server.

HTTP works on top of the **Internet Protocol** (**IP**). In this protocol, machines are addressed using an IP address, which makes it possible to communicate between different **local area networks** (**LANs**) that might use different addressing schemes, even though the most common ones are Ethernet-type networks that use **media access control** (**MAC**) addresses. Communication in HTTP is then done over a **Transmission Control Protocol** (**TCP**) connection between the client and the server. The TCP connection makes sure that the packets are not lost and are received in the same order in which they were sent. The connection endpoints are defined by the corresponding IP addresses and a corresponding port number. The assigned default port number for HTTP is 80, but other port numbers can also be used; the alternative HTTP port 8080 is common.

 To simplify communication, **Domain Name System** (**DNS**) servers provide a mechanism of using host names instead of IP addresses when referencing a machine on the IP network.

Encryption can done through the use of **Secure Sockets Layer** (**SSL**) or **Transport Layer Security** (**TLS**). When this is done, the protocol is normally named **Hypertext Transfer Protocol Secure** (**HTTPS**) and the communication is performed on a separate port, normally 443. In this case, most commonly the server, but also the client, can be authenticated using X.509 certificates that are based on a **Public Key Infrastructure** (**PKI**), where anybody with access to the public part of the certificate can encrypt data meant for the holder of the private part of the certificate. The private part is required to decrypt the information. These certificates allow the validation of the domain of the server or the identity of the client. They also provide a means to check who their issuer is and whether the certificates are invalid because they have been revoked. The Internet architecture is shown in the following diagram:

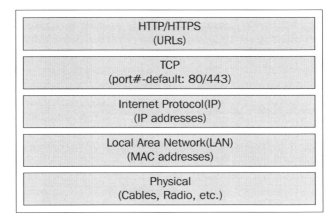

*The HTTP Protocol*

HTTP is a cornerstone of **service-oriented architecture** (**SOA**), where methods for publishing services through HTTP are called web services. One important manner of publishing web services is called **Simple Object Access Protocol (SOAP)**, where web methods, their arguments, return values, bindings, and so on, are encoded in a specific XML format. It is then documented using the **Web Services Description Language** (**WSDL**). Another popular method of publishing web services is called **Representational State Transfer** (**REST**). This provides a simpler, loosely-coupled architecture where methods are implemented based on the normal HTTP methods and URL query parameters, instead of encoding them in XML using SOAP.

Recent developments based on the use of HTTP include Linked Data; a re-abstraction of the Web, where any type of data can be identified using a **Unique Resource Identifier** (**URI**), semantic representation of this data into Semantic Triples, as well as semantic data formats such as **Resource Description Framework** (**RDF**), readable by machines, or **Terse RDF Triple Language** (**TURTLE**), more readily readable by humans. While the collection of HTTP-based Internet resources is called the Web, these later efforts are known under the name 'the semantic web'.

For a thorough review of HTTP, please see *Appendix E, Fundamentals of HTTP*.

# Adding HTTP support to the sensor

We are now ready to add web support to our working sensor, which we prepared in the previous chapter, and publish its data using the HTTP protocol. The following are the three basic strategies that one can use when publishing data using HTTP:

- In the first strategy the sensor is a client who publishes information to a server on the Internet. The server acts as a broker and informs the interested parties about sensor values. This pattern is called **publish/subscribe**, and it will be discussed later in this book. It has the advantage of simplifying handling events, but it makes it more difficult to get momentary values. Sensors can also be placed behind firewalls, as long as the server is publically available on the Internet.

- Another way is to let all entities in the network be both clients and servers, depending on what they need to do. This pattern will be discussed in *Chapter 3, The UPnP Protocol*. This reduces latency in communication, but requires all participants to be on the same side of any firewalls.

- The method we will employ in this chapter is to let the sensor become an HTTP server, and anybody who is interested in knowing the status of the sensor become the clients. This is advantageous as getting momentary values is easy but sending events is more difficult. It also allows easy access to the sensor from the parties behind firewalls if the sensor is publically available on the Internet.

## Setting up an HTTP server on the sensor

Setting up an HTTP server on the sensor is simple if you are using the Clayster libraries. In the following sections, we will demonstrate with images how to set up an HTTP server and publish different kinds of data such as XML, **JavaScript Object Notation (JSON)**, **Resource Description Framework (RDF)**, **Terse RDF Triple Language** (**TURTLE**), and HTML. However, before we begin, we need to add references to namespaces in our application. Add the following code at the top, since it is needed to be able to work with XML, text, and images:

```
using System.Xml;
using System.Text;
using System.IO;
using System.Drawing;
```

Then, add references to the following Clayster namespaces, which will help us to work with HTTP and the different content types mentioned earlier:

```
using Clayster.Library.Internet;
using Clayster.Library.Internet.HTTP;
using Clayster.Library.Internet.HTML;
using Clayster.Library.Internet.MIME;
using Clayster.Library.Internet.JSON;
using Clayster.Library.Internet.Semantic.Turtle;
using Clayster.Library.Internet.Semantic.Rdf;
using Clayster.Library.IoT;
using Clayster.Library.IoT.SensorData;
using Clayster.Library.Math;
```

The `Internet` library helps us with communication and encoding, the `IoT` library with interoperability, and the `Math` library with graphs.

During application initialization, we will first tell the libraries that we do not want the system to search for and use proxy servers (first parameter), and that we don't lock these settings (second parameter). Proxy servers force HTTP communication to pass through them. This makes them useful network tools and allows an added layer of security and monitoring. However. unless you have one in your network, it can be annoying during application development if the application has to always look for proxy servers in the network when none exist. This also causes a delay during application initialization, because other HTTP communication is paused until the search times out. Application initialization is done using the following code:

```
HttpSocketClient.RegisterHttpProxyUse (false, false);
```

To instantiate an HTTP server, we add the following code before application initialization ends and the main loop begins:

```
HttpServer HttpServer = new HttpServer (80, 10, true, true, 1);
Log.Information ("HTTP Server receiving requests on port " +
   HttpServer.Port.ToString ());
```

This opens a small HTTP server on port 80, which requires the application to be run with *superuser* privileges, which maintains a connection backlog of 10 simultaneous connection attempts, allows both GET and POST methods, and allocates one working thread to handle synchronous web requests. The HTTP server can process both synchronous and asynchronous web resources:

- A synchronous web resource responds within the HTTP handler we register for each resource. These are executed within the context of a working thread.
- An asynchronous web resource handles processing outside the context of the actual request and is responsible for responding by itself. This is not executed within the context of a working thread.

For now, we will focus on synchronous web resources and leave asynchronous web resources for later.

Now we are ready to register web resources on the server. We will create the following web resources:

```
HttpServer.Register ("/", HttpGetRoot, false);
HttpServer.Register ("/html", HttpGetHtml, false);
HttpServer.Register ("/historygraph", HttpGetHistoryGraph, false);
HttpServer.Register ("/xml", HttpGetXml, false);
HttpServer.Register ("/json", HttpGetJson, false);
HttpServer.Register ("/turtle", HttpGetTurtle, false);
HttpServer.Register ("/rdf", HttpGetRdf, false);
```

These are all registered as synchronous web resources that do not require authentication (the third parameter in each call). We will handle authentication later in this chapter. Here, we have registered the path of each resource and connected that path with an HTTP handler method, which will process each corresponding request.

In the previous example, we chose to register web resources using methods that will return the corresponding information dynamically. It is also possible to register web resources based on the `HttpServerSynchronousResource` and `HttpServerAsynchronousResource` classes and implement the functionality as an override of the existing methods. In addition, it is also possible to register static content, either in the form of embedded resources using the `HttpServerEmbeddedResource` class or in the form of files in the filesystem using the `HttpServerResourceFolder` class. In our examples, however, we've chosen to only register resources that generate dynamic content.

We also need to correctly dispose of our server when the application ends, or the application will not be terminated correctly. This is done by adding the following disposal method call in the termination section of the main application:

```
HttpServer.Dispose ();
```

## Setting up an HTTPS server on the sensor

If we want to add an HTTPS support to the application, we will need an `X.509Certificate` with a valid private key. First, we will have to load this certificate to the server's memory. For this, we will need its password, which can be obtained through the following code:

```
X509Certificate2 Certificate =
   new X509Certificate2 ("Certificate.pfx", "PASSWORD");
```

We then create the HTTPS server in a way similar to the HTTP server that we just created, except we will now also tell the server to use SSL/TLS (sixth parameter) and not the client certificates (seventh parameter) and provide the server certificate to use in HTTPS:

```
HttpServer HttpsServer =
   new HttpServer (443, 10, true, true, 1, true, false, Certificate);
Log.Information ("HTTPS Server receiving requests on port " +
   HttpsServer.Port.ToString ());
```

We will then make sure that the same resources that are registered on the HTTP server are also registered on the HTTPS server:

```
foreach (IHttpServerResource Resource in
  HttpServer.GetResources())
    HttpsServer.Register (Resource);
```

We will also need to correctly dispose of the HTTPS server when the application ends, just as we did in the case of the HTTP server. As usual, we will do this in the termination section of the main application, as follows:

```
HttpsServer.Dispose ();
```

## Adding a root menu

The first web resource we will add is a root menu, which is accessible through the path /. It will return an HTML page with links to what can be seen on the device. We will add the root menu method as follows:

```
private static void HttpGetRoot (HttpServerResponse resp,
  HttpServerRequest req)
{
  networkLed.High ();
  try
  {
    resp.ContentType = "text/html";
    resp.Encoding = System.Text.Encoding.UTF8;
    resp.ReturnCode = HttpStatusCode.Successful_OK;
  } finally
  {
    networkLed.Low ();
  }
}
```

This preceding method still does not return any page.

This is because the method header contains the HTTP response object `resp`, and the response should be written to this parameter. The original request can be found in the `req` parameter. Notice the use of the `networkLed` digital output in a try-finally block to signal web access to one of our resources. This pattern will be used throughout this book.

Before responding to the query, the method has to inform the recipient what kind of response it will receive. This is done by setting the ContentType parameter of the response object. If we return an HTML page, we use the Internet media type text/html here. Since we send text back, we also have to choose a text encoding. We choose the UTF8 encoding, which is common on the Web. We also make sure to inform the client, that the operation was successful, and that the OK status code (200) is returned.

We will now return the actual HTML page, a very crude one, having the following code:

```
resp.Write ("<html><head><title>Sensor</title></head>");
resp.Write ("<body><h1>Welcome to Sensor</h1>");
resp.Write ("<p>Below, choose what you want to do.</p><ul>");
resp.Write ("<li>View Data</li><ul>");
resp.Write ("<li><a href='/xml?Momentary=1'>");
resp.Write ("View data as XML using REST</a></li>");
resp.Write ("<li><a href='/json?Momentary=1'>");
resp.Write ("View data as JSON using REST</a></li>");
resp.Write ("<li><a href='/turtle?Momentary=1'>");
resp.Write ("View data as TURTLE using REST</a></li>");
resp.Write ("<li><a href='/rdf?Momentary=1'>");
resp.Write ("View data as RDF using REST</a></li>");
resp.Write ("<li><a href='/html'>");
resp.Write ("Data in a HTML page with graphs</a></li></ul>");
resp.Write ("</body></html>");
```

And then we are done! The previous code will show the following view in a browser when navigating to the root:

**Welcome to Sensor**

Below, choose what you want to do.

- View Data
    - View data as XML using REST
    - View data as JSON using REST
    - View data as TURTLE using REST
    - View data as RDF using REST
    - Data in a HTML page with graphs

# Displaying measured information in an HTML page

We are now ready to display our measured information to anybody through a web page (or HTML page). We've registered the path /html to an HTTP handler method named HttpGetHtml. We will now start implementing it, as follows:

```
private static void HttpGetHtml (HttpServerResponse resp,
  HttpServerRequest req)
{
  networkLed.High ();
  try
  {
    resp.ContentType = "text/html";
    resp.Encoding = System.Text.Encoding.UTF8;
    resp.Expires = DateTime.Now;
    resp.ReturnCode = HttpStatusCode.Successful_OK;
    lock (synchObject)
    {
    }
  }
  finally
  {
    networkLed.Low ();
  }
}
```

The only difference here, compared to the previous method, is that we have added a property to the response: an expiry date and time. Since our values are momentary and are updated every second, we will tell the client that the page expires immediately. This ensures the page is not cached on the client side, and it is reloaded properly when the user wants to see the page again. We also added a lock statement, using our synchronization object, to make sure that access to the momentary values are only available from one thread at a time.

We can now start to return our momentary values, from within the lock statement:

```
resp.Write ("<html><head>");
resp.Write ("<meta http-equiv='refresh' content='60'/>");
resp.Write ("<title>Sensor Readout</title></head>");
resp.Write ("<body><h1>Readout, ");
resp.Write (DateTime.Now.ToString ());
resp.Write ("</h1><table><tr><td>Temperature:</td>");
resp.Write ("<td style='width:20px'/><td>");
```

```
resp.Write (HtmlUtilities.Escape (temperatureC.ToString ("F1")));
resp.Write (" C</td></tr><tr><td>Light:</td><td/><td>");
resp.Write (HtmlUtilities.Escape (lightPercent.ToString ("F1")));
resp.Write (" %</td></tr><tr><td>Motion:</td><td/><td>");
resp.Write (motionDetected.ToString ());
resp.Write ("</td></tr></table>");
```

We would like to draw your attention to the `meta` tag at the top of an HTML document. This tag tells the client to refresh the page every 60 seconds. So, by using this `meta` tag, the page automatically updates itself every minute when it is kept open.

Historical data is best displayed using graphs. To do this, we will output image tags with references to our `historygraph` web resource, as follows:

```
if (perSecond.Count > 1)
{
  resp.Write ("<h2>Second Precision</h2>");
  resp.Write ("<table><tr><td>");
  resp.Write ("<img src='historygraph?p=temp&base=sec&");
  resp.Write ("w=350&h=250' width='480' height='320'/></td>");
  resp.Write ("<td style='width:20px'/><td>");
  resp.Write ("<img src='historygraph?p=light&base=sec&");
  resp.Write ("w=350&h=250' width='480' height='320'/></td>");
  resp.Write ("<td style='width:20px'/><td>");
  resp.Write ("<img src='historygraph?p=motion&base=sec&");
  resp.Write ("w=350&h=250' width='480' height='320'/></td>");
  resp.Write ("</tr></table>");
```

Here, we have used query parameters to inform the `historygraph` resource what we want it to draw. The `p` parameter defines the parameter, the `base` parameter the time base, and the `w` and `h` parameters the width and height respectively of the resulting graph. We will now do the same for minutes, hours, days, and months by assigning the base query parameter the values `min`, `h`, `day` and `month` respectively.

We will then close all `if` statements and terminate the HTML page before we send it to the client:

```
}
resp.Write ("</body><html>");
```

*The HTTP Protocol*

# Generating graphics dynamically

Before we can view the page, we also need to create our `historygraph` resource that will generate the graph images referenced from the HTML page. We will start by defining the method in our usual way:

```
private static void HttpGetHistoryGraph (HttpServerResponse resp,
  HttpServerRequest req)
{
  networkLed.High ();
  try
  {
  }
  finally
  {
    networkLed.Low ();
  }
}
```

Within the `try` section of our method, we start by parsing the query parameters of the request. If we find any errors in the request that cannot be mended or ignored, we make sure to throw an `HttpException` exception by taking the `HTTPStatusCode` value and illustrating the error as a parameter. This causes the correct error response to be returned to the client. We start by parsing the width and height of the image to be generated:

```
int Width, Height;

if (!req.Query.TryGetValue ("w", out s) ||
  !int.TryParse (s, out Width) || Width <= 0 || Width > 2048)
    throw new HttpException (HttpStatusCode.ClientError_BadRequest);
if (!req.Query.TryGetValue ("h", out s) ||
  !int.TryParse (s, out Height) || Height <= 0 || Height > 2048)
    throw new HttpException (HttpStatusCode.ClientError_BadRequest);
```

Then we extract the parameter to plot the graph. The parameter is stored in the `p` query parameter. From this value, we will extract the property name corresponding to the parameter in our `Record` class and the `ValueAxis` title in the graph. To do this, we will first define some variables:

```
string ValueAxis;
string ParameterName;
string s;
```

We will then extract the value of the `p` parameter:

```
if (!req.Query.TryGetValue ("p", out s))
  throw new HttpException (HttpStatusCode.ClientError_BadRequest);
```

We will then look at the value of this parameter to deduce the Record property name and the ValueAxis title:

```
switch (s)
{
  case "temp":
    ParameterName = "TemperatureC";
    ValueAxis = "Temperature (C)";
    break;
  case "light":
    ParameterName = "LightPercent";
    ValueAxis = 'Light (%)";
    break;
  case "motion":
    ParameterName = "Motion";
    ValueAxis = 'Motion";
    break;
  default:
    throw new HttpException
      (HttpStatusCode.ClientError_BadRequest);
}
```

We will need to extract the value of the base query parameter to know what time base should be graphed:

```
if (!req.Query.TryGetValue ("base", out s))
  throw new HttpException (HttpStatusCode.ClientError_BadRequest);
```

In the Clayster.Library.Math library, there are tools to generate graphs. These tools can, of course, be accessed programmatically if desired. However, since we already use the library, we can also use its scripting capabilities, which make it easier to create graphs. Variables accessed by script are defined in a Variables collection. So, we need to create one of these:

```
Variables v = new Variables();
```

We also need to tell the client for how long the graph will be valid or when the graph will expire. So, we will need the current date and time:

```
DateTime Now = DateTime.Now;
```

Access to any historical information must be done within a thread-safe critical section of the code. To achieve this, we will use our synchronization object again:

```
lock (synchObject)
{
}
```

Within this critical section, we can now safely access our historical data. It is only the `List<T>` objects that we need to protect and not the `Records` objects. So, as soon as we've populated the `Variables` collection with the arrays returned using the `ToArray()` method, we can unlock our synchronization object again. The following switch statement needs to be executed in the critical section:

```
switch (s)
{
  case "sec":
    v ["Records"] = perSecond.ToArray ();
    resp.Expires = Now;
    break;

  case "min":
    v ["Records"] = perMinute.ToArray ();
    resp.Expires = new DateTime (Now.Year, Now.Month,
    Now.Day, Now.Hour, Now.Minute, 0).AddMinutes (1);
    break;
```

The hour, day, and month cases (`h`, `day`, and `month` respectively) will be handled analogously. We will also make sure to include a default statement that returns an HTTP error, making sure bad requests are handled properly:

```
  default:
    throw new HttpException (
      HttpStatusCode.ClientError_BadRequest);
}
```

Now, the `Variables` collection contains a variable called `Records` that contains an array of `Record` objects to draw. Furthermore, the `ParameterName` variable contains the name of the value property to draw. The `Timestamp` property of each `Record` object contains values for the time axis. Now we have everything we need to plot the graph. We only need to choose the type of graph to plot.

The motion detector reports Boolean values. Plotting the motion values using lines or curves may just cause a mess if it regularly reports motion and non-motion. A better option is perhaps the use of a scatter graph, where each value is displayed using a small colored disc (say, of radius 5 pixels). We interpret false values to be equal to `0` and paint them `Blue`, and true values to be equal to `1` and paint them `Red`.

The Clayster script to accomplish this would be as follows:

```
scatter2d(Records.Timestamp,
   if (Values:=Records.Motion) then 1 else 0,5,
   if Values then 'Red' else 'Blue','','Motion')
```

The other two properties are easier to draw since they can be drawn as simple line graphs:

```
line2d(Records.Timestamp,Records.Property,'Value Axis')
```

The `Expression` class handles parsing and evaluation of Clayster script expressions. This class has two static methods for parsing an expression: `Parse()` and `ParseCached()`. If the expressions are from a limited set of expressions, `ParseCached()` can be used. It only parses an expression once and remembers it. If expressions contain a random component, `Parse()` should be used since caching does not fulfill any purpose except exhausting the server memory.

The parsed expression has an `Evaluate()` method that can be used to evaluate the expression. The method takes a `Variables` collection, which represents the variables available to the expression when evaluating it. All graphical functions return an object of the `Graph` class. This object can be used to generate the image we want to return. First, we need a `Graph` variable to store our script evaluation result:

```
Graph Result;
```

We will then generate, parse, and evaluate our script, as follows:

```
if (ParameterName == "Motion")
  Result = Expression.ParseCached ("scatter2d("+
    "Records.Timestamp, "+
    "if (Values:=Records.Motion) then 1 else 0,5, "+
    "if Values then 'Red' else 'Blue','','Motion')").
    Evaluate (v) as Graph;
else
  Result = Expression.ParseCached ("line2d("+
    "Records.Timestamp,Records." + ParameterName +
    ",'','" + ValueAxis + "')").Evaluate (v)as Graph;
```

We now have our graph. All that is left to do is to generate a bitmapped image from it, to return to the client. We will first get the bitmapped image, as follows:

```
Image Img = Result.GetImage (Width, Height);
```

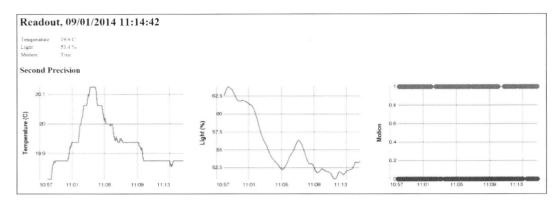
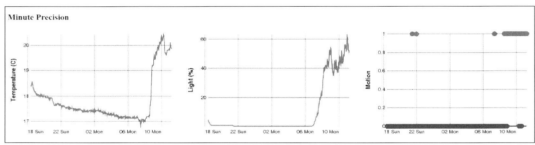
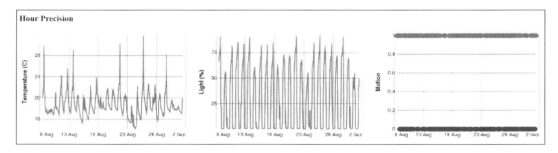

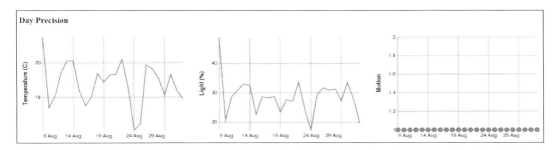

Then we need to encode it so that it can be sent to the client. This is done using **Multi-Purpose Internet Mail Extensions (MIME)** encoding of the image. We can use `MimeUtilities` to encode the image, as follows:

```
byte[] Data = MimeUtilities.Encode (Img, out s);
```

The `Encode()` method on `MimeUtilities` returns a byte array of the encoded object. It also returns the Internet media type or content type that is used to describe how the object was encoded. We tell the client the content type that was used, and that the operation was performed successfully. We then return the binary block of data representing our image, as follows:

```
resp.ContentType = s;
resp.ReturnCode = HttpStatusCode.Successful_OK;
resp.WriteBinary (Data);
```

We can now view our /html page and see not only our momentary values at the top but also graphs displaying values per second, per minute, per hour, per day, and per month, depending on how long we let the sensor work and collect data. At this point, data is not persisted, so as soon as the data is reset, the sensor will lose all the history.

## Creating sensor data resources

We have now created interfaces to display sensor data to humans, and are now ready to export the same sensor data to machines. We have registered four web resources to export sensor data to four different formats with the same names: /xml, /json, /turtle, and /rdf. Luckily, we don't have to write these export methods explicitly as long as we export the sensor data. `Clayster.Library.IoT` helps us to export sensor data to these different formats through the use of an interface named `ISensorDataExport`.

We will create our four web resources, one for each data format. We will begin with the resource that exports XML data:

```
private static void HttpGetXml (HttpServerResponse resp,
  HttpServerRequest req)
{
  HttpGetSensorData (resp, req, "text/xml",
    new SensorDataXmlExport (resp.TextWriter));
}
```

We can use the same code to export data to different formats by replacing the key arguments, as shown in the following table:

| Format | Method | Content Type | Export class |
|---|---|---|---|
| XML | HttpGetXml | text/xml | SensorDataXmlExport |
| JSON | HttpGetJson | application/json | SensorDataJsonExport |
| TURTLE | HttpGetTurtle | text/turtle | SensorDataTurtleExport |
| RDF | HttpGetRdf | application/rdf+xml | SensorDataRdfExport |

## Interpreting the readout request

`Clayster.Library.IoT` can also help the application to interpret query parameters for sensor data queries in an interoperable manner. This is done by using objects of the `ReadoutRequest` class, as follows:

```
private static void HttpGetSensorData (HttpServerResponse resp,
  HttpServerRequest req, string ContentType, ISensorDataExport
  ExportModule)
{
  ReadoutRequest Request = new ReadoutRequest (req);
  HttpGetSensorData (resp, ContentType, ExportModule, Request);
}
```

Often, as in our case, a sensor or a meter has a lot of data. It is definitely not desirable to return all the data to everybody who requests information. In our case, the sensor can store up to 5000 records of historical information. So, why should we export all this information to somebody who only wants to see the momentary values? We shouldn't. The `ReadoutRequest` class in the `Clayster.Library.IoT.SensorData` namespace helps us to parse a sensor data request query in an interoperable fashion and lets us know the type of data that is requested. It helps us determine which field names to report on which nodes. It also helps us to limit the output to specific readout types or a specific time interval. In addition, it provides all external credentials used in distributed transactions. *Appendix F, Sensor Data Query Parameters*, provides a detailed explanation of the query parameters that are used by the `ReadoutRequest` class.

# Testing our data export

Data export is now complete, and so the next step is to test the different data formats and see what they look like. First, we will test our XML data export using an URL similar to the following:

`http://192.168.0.29/xml?Momentary=1&HistoricalDay=1&Temperature=1`

This will only read momentary and daily historical-temperature values. Data will come in an unformatted manner, but viewing the data in a browser provides some form of formatting. If we want JSON instead of XML, we must call the `/json` resource instead:

`http://192.168.0.29/json?Momentary=1&HistoricalDay=1&Temperature=1`

The data that is returned can be formatted using online JSON formatting tools to get a better overview of its structure. To test the TURTLE and RDF versions of the data export, we just need to use the URLs similar to the following:

`http://192.168.0.29/turtle?Momentary=1&HistoricalDay=1&Temperature=1`

`http://192.168.0.29/rdf?Momentary=1&HistoricalDay=1&Temperature=1`

> If you've setup HTTPS on your device, you access the resources using the https URI scheme instead of the http URI scheme.

# User authentication

Publishing things on the Internet is risky. Anybody with access to the thing might also try to use it with malicious intent. For this reason, it is important to protect all public interfaces with some form of user authentication mechanism to make sure only approved users with correct privileges are given access to the device.

> As discussed in the introduction to HTTP, there are several types of user authentication mechanisms to choose from. High-value entities are best protected using both server-side and client-side certificates over an encrypted connection (HTTPS). Although this book does not necessarily deal with things of high individual value, some form of protection is still needed.

We have two types of authentication:

- The first is the www authentication mechanism provided by the HTTP protocol itself. This mechanism is suitable for automation
- The second is a login process embedded into the web application itself, and it uses sessions to maintain user login credentials

Both of these will be explained in *Appendix G, Security in HTTP*.

# Adding events for enhanced network performance

Earlier we had a discussion about the positive and negative aspects of letting the sensor be an HTTP server. One of the positive aspects is that it is very easy for others to get current information when they want. However, it is difficult for the sensor to inform interested parties when something happens. If we would have let the sensor act as a HTTP client instead, the roles would have been reversed. It would have been easy to inform others when something happens, but it would have been difficult for interested parties to get current information when they wanted it.

Since we have chosen to let the sensor be an HTTP server, *Appendix H, Delayed Responses in HTTP*, is dedicated to show how we can inform interested parties of events that occur on the device and when they occur, without the need for constant polling of the device. This architecture will lend itself naturally to a subscription pattern, where different parties can subscribe to different types of events in a natural fashion. These event resources will be used later by the controller to receive information when critical events occur, without the need to constantly poll the sensor.

# Adding HTTP support to the actuator

In automation, apart from having a normal web interface, it is important to be able to provide interoperable interfaces for control. One of the simplest methods to achieve this is through web services. This section shows you how to add support to an application for web services that support both SOAP and REST.

# Creating the web services resource

A web services resource is a special type of synchronous web resource. Instead of you parsing a query string or decode data in the response, the web service engine does that for you. All you need to do is create methods as you normally do, perhaps with some added documentation, and the web service engine will publish these methods using both SOAP and REST. Before we define our web service, we need the references to `System.Web` and `System.Web.Services` in our application. We also need to add a namespace reference to our application:

```
using System.Web.Services;
```

We will define a web service resource by creating a class that derives from `HttpServerWebService`. Apart from providing the path of the web service locally on the HTTP server, you also need to define a namespace for the web service. This namespace defines the interface and web services with the same namespace, even though they are hosted on different servers, and are supposed to be interoperable. This can be seen in the following code:

```
private class WebServiceAPI : HttpServerWebService
{
  public WebServiceAPI ()
  : base ("/ws")
  {
  }
  public override string Namespace
  {
    get
    {
      return "http://clayster.com/learniot/actuator/ws/1.0/";
    }
  }
}
```

The web service engine can help you test your web services by creating test forms for them. Normally, these test forms are only available if you navigate to the web service from the same machine. Since we also work with Raspberry Pi boards from remote computers, we must explicitly activate test forms even for remote requests. However, as soon as we do not need these test forms, they should be made inaccessible from the remote machines. We can activate test forms by using the following property override:

```
public override bool CanShowTestFormOnRemoteComputers
{
  get
```

```
    {
      return true;
    }
}
```

Since web services are used for control and can cause problems if accessed by malicious users, it is important that we register the resource enabling authentication. This is important once the test forms have been activated. We can register the web services activating authentication, as follows:

```
HttpServer.Register (new WebServiceAPI (), true);
```

## Accessing individual outputs

Let's begin to create web service methods. We will start with methods for control of individual outputs. For instance, the following method will allow us to get the output status of one specific digital output:

```
[WebMethod]
[WebMethodDocumentation
  ("Returns the current status of the digital output.")]
public bool GetDigitalOutput
  ([WebMethodParameterDocumentation
  ("Digital Output Number. Possible values are 1 to 8.")]int Nr)
{
  if (Nr >= 1 && Nr <= 8)
    return digitalOutputs [Nr - 1].Value;
  else
    return false;
}
```

The `WebMethod` attribute tells the web service engine that this method should be published, and it can be accessed through the web service. To help the consumer of the web service, we should also provide documentation on how the web service works. This is done by adding the `WebMethodDocumentation` attributes on each method, and the `WebMethodParameterDocumentation` attributes in each input parameter. This documentation will be displayed in test forms and WSDL documents describing the web service.

We will also create a method for setting an individual output, as follows:

```
[WebMethod]
[WebMethodDocumentation
  ("Sets the value of a specific digital output.")]
public void SetDigitalOutput (
  [WebMethodParameterDocumentation (
  "Digital Output Number. Possible values are 1 to 8.")]
  int Nr,

  [WebMethodParameterDocumentation ("Output State to set.")]
  bool Value)
{
  if (Nr >= 1 && Nr <= 8)
  {
    digitalOutputs [Nr - 1].Value = Value;
    state.SetDO (Nr, Value);
    state.UpdateIfModified ();
  }
}
```

## Collective access to outputs

The web services class also provides web methods for setting and getting all digital outputs at once. Here, the digital outputs are encoded into one byte, where each output corresponds to one bit (DO1=bit 0 … DO8=bit 7). The following methods are implemented analogously with the previous method:

```
public byte GetDigitalOutputs ();
public void SetDigitalOutputs (byte Values);
```

## Accessing the alarm output

In the same way, the following two web methods are published for getting and setting the state of the alarm output:

```
public bool GetAlarmOutput ();
public void SetAlarmOutput ();
```

*The HTTP Protocol*

# Using the test form

To access the test form of a web service, we only need to browse to the resource using a browser. In our case, the path of our web service is /ws; so, if the IP address of our Raspberry Pi is 192.168.0.23, we only need to go to http://192.168.0.23/ws and we will see something similar to the following in the browser:

**Actuator.MainClass+WebServiceAPI**

- GetDigitalOutput
- SetDigitalOutput
- GetDigitalOutputs
- SetDigitalOutputs
- GetAlarmOutput
- SetAlarmOutput

The main page of the web service will contain links to each method published by the service. Clicking on any of the methods will open the test form for that web method in a separate tab. The following image shows the test form for the **SetDigitalOutput** web method:

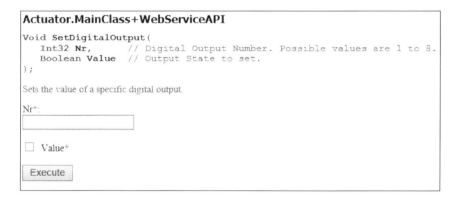

You will notice that the web service documentation that we added to the method and its parameters are displayed in the test form. Since no default value attributes were added to any of the parameters, all parameters are required. This is indicated on the image by a red asterisk against each parameter. If you want to specify default values for parameters, you can use any of the available WebMethodParameterDefault* attributes.

When you click on the **Execute** button, the method will be executed and a new tab will open that will contain the response of the call. If the web method has a return type set as void, the new tab will simply be blank. Otherwise, the return type will contain a SOAP message encoded using XML.

## Accessing WSDL

The SOAP web service interface is documented in what is called a **Web Service Definition Language** (**WSDL**) document. This document is automatically generated by the web services engine. You can access it through the same URL through which you would access the test form by adding ?wsdl at the end (http://192.168.0.23/ws?wsdl).

By using this WSDL you can use development tools to automatically create code to access your web service. You can also use web service test tools like SoapUI to test and automate your web services in a simple manner. You can download and test SoapUI at http://www.soapui.org/.

## Using the REST web service interface

The web services that we created earlier can also be accessed using a REST-like web service interface. This is done by using a HTTP GET operation on the web service resource, where the parameters are encoded as query parameters in the URL. A special query parameter named op is used to identify the method. For example, to set output number five, we only have to perform an HTTP GET operation similar to the following URL:

http://192.168.0.23/ws?op=SetDigitalOutput&Nr=5&Value=1

If the web service has optional parameters, which means there are parameters that have default values defined for them, then these do not need to be present in the URL. If they are not present, they will receive the default values defined for them in the code.

> The method of using HTTP GET to perform control operations might not work as expected if clients or in-between proxies cache the result. This might happen if multiple requests are issued quickly. The response will be clearly marked not to be cached, but some clients and proxies might ignore this fact since the HTTP GET operation is assumed to be idempotent, which means that the same method call twice is assumed to be equal to just one method call. If this is a concern, the POST method should always be used. If using relative-value arguments (like Increase By) instead of absolute-value arguments (like Set to), this is the case. The GET method, however, provides an exceptionally easy way to test and use a service.

## Adding HTTP support to the controller

We now have a sensor and an actuator that speaks HTTP. To tie these together, we also need to add HTTP to the controller. The controller will act as an HTTP client, as opposed to our previous examples where each application acted as an HTTP server. We will use the `HttpSocketClient` class to access the web resources provided by the sensor. We will create our connection to our sensor, as follows:

```
HttpSocketClient HttpClient;
HttpClient = new HttpSocketClient ("192.168.0.29", 80,
  new DigestAuthentication ("Peter", "Waher"));
HttpClient.ReceiveTimeout = 30000;
HttpClient.Open ();
```

Here, we will add the client-side version of the digest authentication scheme found in `Clayster.Library.Internet.HTTP.ClientCredentials`. We will also specify a timeout of 30,000 milliseconds since we will use the even subscription mechanism of retrieving data from the sensor.

To get data from the sensor is easy. All that is needed to do is get the XML using the `GET` method and call the `UpdateFields()` method described in the previous chapter, to parse the XML and flag any corresponding control actions:

```
HttpResponse Response = HttpClient.GET (Resource);
Xml = Response.Xml;
if (UpdateFields (Xml))
{
  hasValues = true;
  CheckControlRules ();
}
```

The first time we access the sensor, we just get the sensor data in the normal way by using the following code:

```
Resource = "/xml?Momentary=1&Light=1&Motion=1";
```

## Subscribing to events

Now that we know the current state of the sensor, we only need to get data from the sensor when it implies a control action change. Instead of constantly polling the sensor using the resource above, we will use the event resources published by the sensor. This is detailed in *Appendix H, Delayed Responses in HTTP*. There are nine different states and by knowing the current control states, we can calculate when these states will change.

States can change when the state of LEDs change, when the motion changes and when the light is below 20 percent. So, we need to check the distance of the light density to one of these three states: when one more LED is lit, when one more LED is unlit, or when the light reaches 20 percent. This can be done with the following code:

```
int NrLeds = (int)System.Math.Round ((8 * lightPercent) / 100);
double LightNextStepDown = 100 * (NrLeds - 0.1) / 8;
double LightNextStepUp = 100 * (NrLeds + 1) / 8;
double DistDown = System.Math.Abs
   (lightPercent - LightNextStepDown);
double DistUp = System.Math.Abs (LightNextStepUp - lightPercent);
double Dist20 = System.Math.Abs (20 - lightPercent);
double MinDist = System.Math.Min
   (System.Math.Min (DistDown, DistUp), Dist20);
```

We will also impose a minimum distance, in case we are very close to a tipping point:

```
if (MinDist < 1)
   MinDist = 1;
```

We can then create the resource string that would let us subscribe to an event from the sensor that is tailored to our needs:

```
StringBuilder sb = new StringBuilder ();
sb.Append ("/event/xml?Light=");
sb.Append (XmlUtilities.DoubleToString (lightPercent, 1));
sb.Append ("&LightDiff=");
sb.Append (XmlUtilities.DoubleToString (MinDist, 1));
sb.Append ("&Motion=");
sb.Append (motion ? "1" : "0");
sb.Append ("&Timeout=25");
Resource = sb.ToString ();
```

We will then put the previous code in the main loop, and keep subscribing to events from the sensor. In turn the sensor will simply wait until the corresponding event occurs or the request times out. If the event subscription times out, the controller will at least get the latest momentary values on which the next event subscription will be based.

A timeout argument is used to tell the client how long it should wait (in seconds) before returning an empty response. Such a timeout is necessary since the underlying TCP connection will be dropped if no communication occurs within a given time period. This time depends on the network and the routers used between the client and the server. When the possibly empty response is returned a new, similar request will be made immediately.

# Creating the control thread

Control of the actuator will be done in a separate thread so that sensor communication is not affected. From the main thread, we can start the control thread, as follows:

```
Thread ControlThread;
ControlThread = new Thread (ControlHttp);
ControlThread.Name = "Control HTTP";
ControlThread.Priority = ThreadPriority.Normal;
ControlThread.Start ();
```

When terminating the application, we will simply abort the thread by calling the `Abort()` method:

```
ControlThread.Abort ();
ControlThread = null;
```

The control thread in itself is a very simple thread. It simply waits for events to occur, based on what happens to the two `AutoResetEvent` objects defined earlier:

```
private static void ControlHttp ()
{
  try
  {
    WaitHandle[] Handles = new WaitHandle[]
      {updateLeds, updateAlarm };
    while (true)
    {
      try
      {
        switch (WaitHandle.WaitAny (Handles, 1000))
        {
        }
      }
      catch (Exception ex)
      {
        Log.Exception (ex);
      }
    }
  }
  catch (ThreadAbortException)
  {
    Thread.ResetAbort ();
  }
  catch (Exception ex)
  {
    Log.Exception (ex);
  }
}
```

The static `WaitHandle.WaitAny()` method waits for an event to occur on any of the event objects available in the array. It returns a zero-based index to the event object that was triggered and a negative value when the operation times out. Only one event object can trigger at the a time. Furthermore, the `AutoResetEvent` objects, as the name implies, auto-reset themselves when they are triggered in the thread. This means that they can be set again from the other thread and trigger a new event.

## Controlling the actuator

The first event object is `updateLeds`. It is set when the LEDs on the actuator needs to be changed. The `lastLedMask` variable contains the state of how the LEDs should be lit. We perform the LED control by using the REST interface on our web service method that we defined earlier:

```
case 0:// Update LEDS
  int i;
  lock (synchObject)
  {
    i = lastLedMask;
  }
  HttpUtilities.GET ("http://Peter:Waher@192.168.0.23/ws/?" +
  "op=SetDigitalOutputs&Values=" + i.ToString ());
  break;
```

Note how it is possible to include the user credentials in the URL directly. `HttpUtilities` will make the corresponding operations necessary to connect, and authenticate itself, and the GET method fetches the contents from the corresponding resource.

The second event object concerns itself with the status of the alarm output. The `lastAlarm` variable contains the desired state of the alarm output. Also, we perform the alarm control using the REST interface to the corresponding web service method defined in the actuator project:

```
case 1:// Update Alarm
  bool b;
  lock (synchObject)
  {
    b = lastAlarm.Value;
  }
  HttpUtilities.GET (http://Peter:Waher@192.168.0.23/ws/?
   + "op=SetAlarmOutput&Value=" + (b ? "true" : "false"));
  break;
```

# Summary

In this chapter, you were provided with a brief overview of the Web and the protocols and components that have been used to build the Web. You have seen how to apply HTTP to sensors, actuators, and controllers. You have also learned how to utilize its strengths and compensate for some of its weaknesses. You have used the request/response pattern and used delayed responses to simulate event notification. You have also applied basic security by authenticating users and maintaining sessions. Finally, you also implemented web services for interoperable automation.

In the next chapter, you will learn about how the HTTP protocol has been extended and used by **Universal Plug and Play (UPnP)** to provide a means for automatic device-and-service discovery and an alternative method for event notification.

# 3
# The UPnP Protocol

**Universal Plug and Play** (**UPnP**) is a protocol or an architecture that uses multiple protocols, helps devices in ad hoc IP networks to discover each other, detects services hosted by each device, and executes actions and reports events. Ad hoc networks are networks with no predefined topology or configuration; here, devices find themselves and adapt themselves to the surrounding environment. UPnP is largely used by consumer electronics in home or office environments. In this chapter, you will learn:

- The basic UPnP device architecture
- How to create a UPnP device and service description documents
- How to implement a UPnP service
- How to discover devices and subscribe to events through them

> All source code presented in this book is available for download. Source code for this chapter and the next, can be downloaded here:
> `https://github.com/Clayster/Learning-IoT-UPnP`

## Introducing UPnP

UPnP is a very common protocol. It is used by almost all network-enabled consumer electronics products used in your home or office, and as such, it is a vital part of **Digital Living Network Alliance (DLNA)**. The standard body for UPnP is the UPnP Forum (`upnp.org`). UPnP is largely based on an HTTP application where both clients and servers are participants. This HTTP is, however, extended so that it can be used over TCP as well as UDP, where both use unicast addressing (HTTPU) and multicast addressing (HTTPMU).

Discovery of devices in the network is performed using **Simple Service Discovery Protocol** (**SSDP**), which is based on HTTP over UDP, and event subscriptions and notifications are based on **General Event Notification Architecture** (**GENA**). Both SSDP and GENA introduce new HTTP methods to search, notify and subscribe to and unsubscribe from an event. Devices find each other by notifying the network of their existence using multicast addressing and the available services. However, they can also search for the network using multicast addressing for certain types of devices or services. Actions on services are called using SOAP web service calls.

## Providing a service architecture

UPnP defines an object hierarchy for UPnP-compliant devices. Each device consists of a **root device**. Each root device can publish zero or more services and embedded devices. Each embedded device can iteratively publish more services and embedded devices by itself. Each service in turn publishes a set of actions and state variables. Actions are methods that can be called on the service using SOAP web service method calls. Actions take a set of arguments. Each argument has a name, direction (if it is input or output), and a state variable reference. From this reference, the data type of the argument is deduced. State variables define the current state of a service, and each one has a name, data type, and variable value. Furthermore, state variables can be normal, evented, and/or multicast-evented. When evented state variables change their value, they are propagated to the network through event messages. Normally, evented state variables are sent only to subscribers who use normal HTTP. Multicast-evented state variables are propagated through multicast HTTPMU NOTIFY messages on the SSDP multicast addresses being used, but using a different port number. There's no need to subscribe to such event variables in order to be kept updated on their values.

## Documenting device and service capabilities

Each UPnP-compatible device in the network is described in a **Device Description Document** (**DDD**), an XML document hosted by the device itself. When the device makes its presence known to the network, it always includes a reference to the location of this document. Interested parties then download the document and any referenced material to learn what type of device this is and how to interact with it. The document includes some basic information understandable by machines, but it also includes information for human interfaces. Finally, the DDD includes references to embedded devices, if any, and references to any services published by the device.

Each service published by a device is described in a standalone **Service Control Protocol Description** (**SCPD**) document, each one an XML document also hosted by the device. Even though SOAP is used to call methods on each service, UPnP-compliant services are drastically reduced in functionality compared to normal SOAP web services. SOAP and WSDL simply give devices too many options, making interoperability a problem. For this reason, a simpler service architecture is used. Instead of using WSDL to describe the service methods, you can use the `scpd.xml` document to do this directly.

For a more detailed introduction to UPnP, please refer to *Appendix I, Fundamentals of UPnP*.

> To be able to develop and test applications for a given protocol, it is often helpful if you have tools available that can be used to test and monitor your progress. For UPnP, one such useful set of tools is available in the Open Source project, "Developer Tools for UPnP technologies". In particular, the Device Spy application is useful to interact with UPnP-compliant devices in your network. You can download these tools and the source code from `http://opentools.homeip.net/dev-tools-for-upnp`.

# Creating a device description document

We are now ready to add support for UPnP to our camera. To begin, we will create a subfolder called UPnP. Here we will put all our UPnP-related files. We will make all these files embedded resources (selecting **Embedded Resource** as the **Build Action** for the corresponding files). This makes the compiler embed the files into the executable file that is generated when the compiler builds the project. The first file we will add to the project is a DDD called `CameraDevice.xml` that represents our root device. Our project will only host one root device. This document is an XML document, and it begins by stating what version of UPnP is used:

```
<?xml version="1.0" encoding="utf-8"?>
<root xmlns="urn:schemas-upnp-org:device-1-0">
  <specVersion>
    <major>1</major>
    <minor>0</minor>
  </specVersion>
```

The next element contains the base URL of the document. All references made in the document will be relative to this base URL. Since we do not know the IP address and port number to be used in the actual camera when it is installed, we put in placeholders instead, which we will replace with the actual values at runtime:

```
<URLBase>http://{IP}:{PORT}</URLBase>
```

## Choosing a device type

This is where the device description begins. It starts with the device type. The device type is actually a URN that uses a specific format:

```
urn:DOMAIN:device:NAME
```

The DOMAIN attribute is replaced by the domain name of the party that creates the interface (with dots replaced by hyphens), and NAME is a unique name, within the namespace of the domain, for the device type. UPnP Forum defines a list of standard device types that can be used. It can be found at http://upnp.org/sdcps-and-certification/standards/sdcps/. Among these, one exists for digital security cameras, the DigitalSecurityCamera:1 interface that can be found at http://upnp.org/specs/ha/UPnP-ha-DigitalSecurityCamera-v1-Device.pdf. The device type URN of this device is urn:schemas-upnp-org:device:DigitalSecurityCamera:1. If we are satisfied with this, we can simply copy the files from the UPnP Forum and continue.

However, when we look at the specification, we notice that there are many items that are not suitable for our project: one optional service interface concerning video, which our camera does not support, and another interface concerning settings. But these settings are not applicable in our case, as our camera does everything for us automatically. We only want to publish pictures taken through the DigitalSecurityCameraStillImage:1 interface.

To be able to create a new device type, albeit based on an existing standardized device type, we need to create our own device type URN and we need to do this using a domain name we have control over. We also need to give it a device type name. We will call our camera learningIoTCamera, and give it a version number, namely 1. We formalize this in our device description document as follows:

```
<deviceType>urn:clayster-com:device:learningIotCamera:1</deviceType>
```

## Being friendly

URNs are machine-readable but difficult to understand for human users. For this reason, we also need to give the device a "friendly" name, meaning a name for human users:

```
<friendlyName>Learning-IoT Camera ({IP})</friendlyName>
```

We then provide some information about the manufacturer of the device:

```
<manufacturer>Clayster</manufacturer>
<manufacturerURL>http://clayster.com/</manufacturerURL>
```

This is followed by some information about the device model:

```
<modelDescription>UPnP Camera sample from the Learning-IoT book.</modelDescription>
<modelName>Learning-IoT Camera</modelName>
<modelNumber>CAM1</modelNumber>
<modelURL>http://clayster.com/learning-iot</modelURL>
```

## Providing the device with an identity

We also need to specify a **Unique Device Name** (**UDN**). This is a number that is unique to each individual device and will be, in our case, a GUID generated by the device during the initial configuration. It will be used by others who interact with the device, and it needs to remain the same even if the device restarts. Since we do not know the ID beforehand, we will put a placeholder that we can replace later in the XML document:

```
<UDN>uuid:{UDN}</UDN>
```

We can also provide a **Universal Product Code** (**UPC**) in the file if we have one. If we don't, we leave the tag empty:

```
<UPC/>
```

## Adding icons

Custom icons are nice, especially if you are used to graphical user interfaces. UPnP devices can publish a varied number of icons in different resolutions so that graphical user interfaces that display the devices in the network in different ways can choose the icon that best suits their needs. In our example, we will choose a freely available camera icon drawn by LeoYue (alias), which can be found at http://www.iconarchive.com/show/the-bourne-ultimatum-icons-by-leoyue/Camera-icon.html.

Then, save this icon in seven different resolutions (16 x 16, 24 x 24, 32 x 32, 48 x 48, 64 x 64, 128 x 128, and 256 x 256) as seven different PNG files in the `UPnP` folder of our project. We make all the image files embedded resources. We then list these icons in the device description document as follows. We only include the first icon here for reference while the other six are analogous and represented by an ellipsis (…):

```
<iconList>
  <icon>
    <mimetype>image/png</mimetype>
    <width>16</width>
    <height>16</height>
    <depth>32</depth>
    <url>/Icon/16x16.png</url>
  </icon>
  …
</iconList>
```

It is worthwhile to mention that the icons have not been published through our web interface yet, but we need to provide relative URLs to the icons. We will have to remember the paths provided to the icons here so that we can make sure we publish them correctly through our web interface later.

# Adding references to services

Following the icons comes the list of services supported by the device. In our case, the list will only contain one service, the `DigitalSecurityCameraStillImage:1` service, published by the UPnP Forum (http://upnp.org/specs/ha/UPnP-ha-StillImage-v1-Service.pdf). We begin by adding both a URN that identifies the service type and another URN that provides a service ID for the service:

```
<serviceType>urn:schemas-upnp-org:service:
  DigitalSecurityCameraStillImage:1</serviceType>
<serviceId>urn:upnp-org:serviceId:
  DigitalSecurityCameraStillImage</serviceId>
```

> In the preceding example, the URNs have been split into two rows for readability. In the actual example, they need to be provided on one line without any whitespace.

We then provide a relative URL to the SCPD document, which we will create shortly:

```
<SCPDURL>
  /StillImageService.xml
</SCPDURL>
```

We also need to provide relative URLs that will be used for control (executing actions on the service) and event subscription. In our example, we will handle both using the same web resource:

```
<controlURL>/StillImage</controlURL>
<eventSubURL>/StillImage</eventSubURL>
```

# Topping off with a URL to a web presentation page

We finish the device description document by providing a relative URL to an HTML page that can be used for web presentation of the device. Here, we list our `/html` web resource:

```
<presentationURL>/html</presentationURL>
```

# Creating the service description document

In our example, we will only implement one service: the DigitalSecurityCameraStillImage:1 interface provided by the UPnP forum (http://upnp.org/specs/ha/UPnP-ha-StillImage-v1-Service.pdf). The service description XML already exists; it is published by the UPnP Forum. However, we still need to create a file in our project that our device can use to publish the SCPD XML document. The file we will create will be called `StillImageService.xml`, and we will put it in the UPnP folder together with the other UPnP-related files. We will also make sure the file is created as an embedded resource of the project.

The service file begins with a specification of the UPnP version that is used:

```
<?xml version="1.0" encoding="utf-8"?>
<scpd xmlns="urn:schemas-upnp-org:service-1-0">
  <specVersion>
    <major>1</major>
    <minor>0</minor>
  </specVersion>
```

## Adding actions

Directly following the version follows a list of actions published by the service. Each action is defined by a name and a list of arguments. Each argument in turn also has a name, a direction, and a reference to a state variable that defines the underlying state variable and the data type being referenced. The first action in our example is defined as follows:

```
<actionList>
  <action>
    <name>GetAvailableEncodings</name>
    <argumentList>
      <argument>
        <name>RetAvailableEncodings</name>
        <direction>out</direction>
        <relatedStateVariable>AvailableEncodings
          </relatedStateVariable>
      </argument>
    </argumentList>
  </action>
</actionList>
```

 The new line added to the `relatedStateVariable` element in the preceding code is only inserted for readability.

## Adding state variables

After having listed all the actions, the corresponding state variables need to be listed. In our example, there will be variables that send events and variables that do not. State variables are defined as follows. Only the first two state variables are listed here:

```
<serviceStateTable>
  <stateVariable sendEvents="no">
    <name>AvailableEncodings</name>
    <dataType>string</dataType>
  </stateVariable>
  <stateVariable sendEvents="yes">
    <name>DefaultEncoding</name>
    <dataType>string</dataType>
  </stateVariable>
</serviceStateTable>
```

When we are done with listing our state variables, we are done with the service document:

```
</scpd>
```

For a list of data types available in UPnP, refer to *Appendix J, Data types in UPnP*.

## Adding a unique device name

We need each device to have a unique identity or UDN. To do this, we add a `udn` property to our `DefaultSettings` class. We initialize the property with a new `GUID` so that the first time the application is run and a new object created, it will receive a new unique `GUID` identifier as `udn`.

```
private string udn = Guid.NewGuid().ToString();
```

The public interface for our property is defined as follows:

```
[DBShortStringClipped (false)]
public string UDN
{
  get
  {
    return this.udn;
  }
  set
  {
    if(this.udn != value)
    {
      this.udn = value;
      this.Modified = true;
    }
  }
}
```

## Providing a web interface

The camera project comes with a web interface that allows us to interact with the camera through a browser. We will use this interface not only to test our camera, but also to link to it from our UPnP interface. To avoid repetition of how to create such web interfaces, only an overview of the web interface is provided here. For a more detailed description of how this web interface is developed, please refer to *Appendix K, Camera Web Interface*.

The web interface has two basic resources. First, the `/html` resource returns HTML that displays the camera, and then we have `/camera`, which returns an image. Both take query parameters. Encoding controls image encoding by providing the Internet media type to use. Compression controls the compression ratio and can be a number between 0 and 255. Resolution controls image resolution and can take one of the three values: 160 x 120, 320 x 240, or 640 x 480. Both resources will be available in a protected and an unprotected version. The protected version will be used in the web interface and requires the user to log in and create a session before the camera can be viewed. The unprotected version, which will be used in the UPnP interface, does not require any user authentication since it is assumed to be accessible only in the local area network.

# Creating a UPnP interface

UPnP is based on HTTP and extensions of HTTP onto UDP. As mentioned earlier, UPnP is originally thought of to work in protected networks where devices communicate with each other, unhindered by firewalls. Since we also aim for our device to be connected to the Internet, we need to create two different HTTP interfaces: one for the Internet that is protected and one for the local area network that is unprotected. The protected interface will work on the standard HTTP port 80, and the UPnP server will, in our case, work on port 8080. This port number is not fixed by any standard; it can be any free port. Port numbers below 1024 will require superuser privileges when you run the application. Since notification of presence is done using multicast UDP, everybody will be aware of the IP and port number to use when communicating with the device. We begin by defining our HTTP server to use for UPnP:

```
private static HttpServer upnpServer;
```

We then create our second HTTP server like we did for our first:

```
upnpServer = new HttpServer(8080, 10, true, true, 1);
Log.Information("UPnP Server receiving requests on port " +
  upnpServer.Port.ToString ());
```

We also publish the web interface through the UPnP interface, but this time with the unprotected version:

```
upnpServer.Register("/", HttpGetRootUnprotected,
  HttpPostRoot, false);
```

When the application closes, we need to dispose of this object too to make sure any threads are closed. Otherwise, the application will not close properly:

```
upnpServer.Dispose();
```

# Registering UPnP resources

Next, we publish our device and service description documents. These are built into the executable file as embedded resources. Each embedded resource has its own unique resource name, which is the namespace of the project. In our case, this is Camera and is followed by a period (.); this is in turn followed by the path of the embedded file where the directory separator (/ or \) is replaced by dots. The service description document requires no changes, so we return it as is. But the device description document requires that we replace placeholders with actual values, so we register a method with the resource to be able to modify the document when requested. This is done as follows:

```
upnpServer.Register("/CameraDevice.xml",
   HttpGetCameraDevice, false);
upnpServer.Register(new HttpServerEmbeddedResource
   ("/StillImageService.xml",
   "Camera.UPnP.StillImageService.xml"));
```

To avoid problems for potential receivers—if you're handling text files as binary files, as is the case with our service file where the content type is set manually (from the file extension in our case)—make sure you save the corresponding files using a text editor that lets you save them without a byte order mark. Alternatively, you can provide a preamble to avoid problems with conflicting encodings. Refer to *Appendix L, Text Encoding on the Web*, for a discussion on the different types of encodings for text content on the Web.

We register the path to our icons in a similar manner. Here, the 16 x 16 icon is registered, and the 24 x 24, 32 x 32, 48 x 48, 64 x 64, 128 x 128, and 256 x 256 are registered in a similar manner:

```
("/Icon/16x16.png", "Camera.UPnP.16x16.png"));
```

In .NET on Windows, filenames that start with a digit, as is the case with the filenames of our icons, get resource names prefixed by underscores (_). This is not the case when you run an application on MONO. If you're running the application on Windows, the resource name for the first icon would be, for instance, Camera.UPnP._16x16.png.

# Replacing placeholders

Our device description document (DDD) contains three placeholders that need to be replaced with actual values: {IP} with the IP address that others can use to reach the device, {PORT} with the port number that we will use while communicating with the device, and finally, {UDN} that has to be replaced by the unique device name generated for our device instance. We start by defining our method as follows:

```
private static void HttpGetCameraDevice (HttpServerResponse resp,
  HttpServerRequest req)
{
  networkLed.High();
  try
  {
```

We then load the XML from our embedded resource into a string that we can modify:

```
    string Xml;
    byte[] Data;
    int c;

    using (Stream stream = Assembly.GetExecutingAssembly ().
    GetManifestResourceStream ("Camera.UPnP.CameraDevice.xml"))
    {
      c = (int)stream.Length;
      Data = new byte[c];
      stream.Position = 0;
      stream.Read(Data, 0, c);
      Xml = TextDecoder.DecodeString (Data,
        System.Text.Encoding.UTF8);
    }
```

We then need to find the IP address of the device to return. This IP address would normally depend on what network interface the request is made on, and the underlying protocol that is being used (for instance, IPv4 or IPv6). Since we are running our application on Raspberry Pi, we assume there is only one network interface, and it'll be great if we find an IP address that matches the same protocol as that of the request:

```
    string HostName = System.Net.Dns.GetHostName ();
    System.Net.IPHostEntry HostEntry =
      System.Net.Dns.GetHostEntry (HostName);

    foreach(System.Net.IPAddress Address in HostEntry.AddressList)
    {
      if(Address.AddressFamily == req.ClientEndPoint.AddressFamily)
```

```
    {
      Xml = Xml.Replace("{IP}", Address.ToString());
      break;
    }
  }
```

Setting up the port number and unique device name is easier. The first is chosen by us; the second is generated during the first execution of the application and is available in our `defaultSettings` object:

```
Xml = Xml.Replace("{PORT}", upnpServer.Port.ToString ());
Xml = Xml.Replace("{UDN}", defaultSettings.UDN);
```

We then returned the finished XML as follows:

```
    resp.ContentType = "text/xml";
    resp.Encoding = System.Text.Encoding.UTF8;
    resp.ReturnCode = HttpStatusCode.Successful_OK;
    resp.Write(Xml);
  }
  finally
  {
    networkLed.Low();
  }
}
```

## Adding support for SSDP

To add support for SSDP, we will also need to add an SSDP client from the `Clayster.Library.Internet.SSDP` library to the `main` class:

```
private static SsdpClient ssdpClient;
```

We then instantiate it after the creation of the UPnP HTTP server:

```
ssdpClient = new SsdpClient(upnpServer, 10,
   true, true, false, false, false, 30);
```

The first parameter connects the SSDP client with our newly created HTTP server, dedicated to UPnP. Any multicast messages sent will have a **time-to-live** (TTL) of 10 router hops. We will activate it for the IPv4 and IPv6 link-local UPnP multicast addresses (the first two true-valued arguments), but not for the IPv6 site-local, organization-local, or global multicast addresses (the following three false-valued arguments). Searching for new devices on the network will be performed every 30 seconds.

# The UPnP Protocol

When the application closes, we need to dispose of this object too to make sure any threads are closed as well. Otherwise, the application will not close properly.

```
ssdpClient.Dispose();
```

We attach event handlers to the SSDP client. The OnNotify event is raised when searching is done and can be used to notify the network of the available interfaces on the device itself. OnDiscovery event is raised when an incoming search request has been received:

```
ssdpClient.OnNotify += OnSsdpNotify;
ssdpClient.OnDiscovery += OnSsdpDiscovery;
```

We will also need to use the random number generator defined for session management to generate random delay times:

```
private static Random gen = new Random ();
```

## Notifying the network

You can notify the network of your presence and service capabilities. This is done by multicasting NOTIFY messages to the network. We can do this from the OnNotify event handler that is called when the SSDP client itself searches the network for devices. In our case, this is done every 30 seconds. We only have two interfaces to publish on the network, and we begin by publishing the interface for the root device:

```
private static void OnSsdpNotify(object Sender,
SsdpNotifyEventArgs e)
  {
  e.SendNotification(DateTime.Now.AddMinutes (30),
  "/CameraDevice.xml", SsdpClient.UpnpRootDevice,
  "uuid:" + defaultSettings.UDN + "::upnp:rootdevice");
```

The first parameter determines the lifetime of the interface. This means clients do not need to fetch a new interface description during the next 30 minutes. We then point to our device description document resource and tell the network that the notification concerns a root device and the unique device name it has. We then publish the service interface:

```
  e.SendNotification (DateTime.Now.AddMinutes (30),
    "/StillImageService.xml", "urn:schemas-upnp-" +
      "org:service:DigitalSecurityCameraStillImage:1",
      "uuid:" + defaultSettings.UDN +
      ":service:DigitalSecurityCameraStillImage:1");
  }
```

In this case, we also state that the service file is valid for 30 minutes. We then point to its resource and tell the network that it concerns a `DigitalSecurityCameraStillImage:1` service and the unique service name it has.

After these two notifications, recipients in the network will note of the presence and capabilities of our camera, even if they do not actively search for it.

## Responding to searches

When a search is performed, it is sent to the network that uses multicast addressing. Anybody listening to the corresponding multicast address will receive the search request. To avoid spam in a large network, with possible packet loss as a result, the search lets clients respond within a random amount of time, provided the response is sent before the given maximum response time elapses. Furthermore, the search can be restricted to certain device types or services types to avoid unwanted responses being sent. Responding to search requests is much like notifying the network about your interfaces, except that you must check whether the corresponding interface is desired and you send the response as a unicast message back to the one who requested it within the time period specified. And if you're sending multiple notifications, it's recommended that you spread them out and send them over the allotted time to avoid bursts.

We begin by analyzing the search request to see whether any of our interfaces are desired, how many and which ones:

```
private static void OnSsdpDiscovery(object Sender,
   SsdpDiscoveryEventArgs e)
{
   int i, c = 0;
   bool ReportDevice = false;
   bool ReportService = false;

   if (e.ReportInterface(SsdpClient.UpnpRootDevice) ||
      e.ReportInterface("urn:clayster:device:learningIotCamera:1"))
   {
      ReportDevice = true;
      c++;
   }

   if (e.ReportInterface("urn:schemas-upnp-org:service:" +
      "DigitalSecurityCameraStillImage:1"))
   {
      ReportService = true;
      c++;
   }
```

We then create a random number of points in the response interval where we will return the responses:

```
double[] k = new double[c];
lock (lastAccessBySessionId)
{
  for (i = 0; i < c; i++)


  k [i] = gen.NextDouble ();
}
```

The random number generator is *not* thread-safe, so we need to make sure that access to it is done from only one thread at a time. Since we use the random number generator defined for session management, we perform the lock on `lastAccessBySessionId`, which is the same object that is locked when the session management generates a random number.

Since we always want the order of interfaces reported to be the same, we need to sort our set of random time points:

```
Array.Sort (k);
i = 0;
```

If our device description document is desired, we start a timer counting down to the first random time point, scaled for the allowed number of seconds to respond, and make sure that the timer elapses only once and reports it to our interface:

```
if(ReportDevice)
{
  System.Timers.Timer t = new System.Timers.Timer (
    e.MaximumWaitTime * 1000 * k[i++] + 1);
  t.AutoReset = false;
  t.Elapsed += (o2, e2) =>
  {
    e.SendResponse (DateTime.Now.AddMinutes (30),
      "/CameraDevice.xml", SsdpClient.UpnpRootDevice, "uuid:" +
      defaultSettings.UDN + "::upnp:rootdevice");
  };
  t.Start ();
}
```

We do the same with our service interface:

```
if (ReportService)
{
  System.Timers.Timer t = new System.Timers.Timer (
    e.MaximumWaitTime * 1000 * k[i++] + 1);
```

```
      t.AutoReset = false;
      t.Elapsed += (o2, e2) =>
      {
        e.SendResponse (DateTime.Now.AddMinutes (30),
          "/StillImageService.xml",
          "urn:schemas-upnp-org:service:" +
          "DigitalSecurityCameraStillImage:1",
          "uuid:" + defaultSettings.UDN +
          ":service:" +
          "DigitalSecurityCameraStillImage:1");
      };
      t.Start ();
   }
}
```

## Implementing the Still Image service

As we have seen, UPnP services use SOAP to call actions published by the service. But instead of using WSDL to describe the service method calls, a **Service Control Protocol Description** (**SCPD**) document is used. Apart from being much more restrictive when it comes to defining web methods, it also has an added feature that is not supported by normal web services: handling of GENA-type events and event subscriptions. When we implement a UPnP web service, we will do so by inheriting the UPnPWebService class defined in the Clayster.Library.Internet.UPnP namespace. This class in turn is inherited from the normal HttpServerWebService class but adds event handling and subscription capabilities to the web service:

```
public class DigitalSecurityCameraStillImage : UPnPWebService
   {
      public DigitalSecurityCameraStillImage()
      : base("/StillImage")
   {
```

## Initializing evented state variables

Still in the constructor of the web service, there are no subscribers to the state variables it publishes. By using the NotifySubscribers method from within the constructor, we don't actually send the state variables to anybody. What we do is inform about the underlying event handling mechanism of the initial values of the existing state variables. This is done as follows:

```
this.NotifySubscribers (
   new KeyValuePair<string, string> ("DefaultResolution",
     MainClass.defaultSettings.Resolution.ToString ().
     Substring (1)),
```

```
    new KeyValuePair<string, string> (
      "DefaultCompressionLevel",
      MainClass.defaultSettings.CompressionLevel.
      ToString ()),
    new KeyValuePair<string, string> ("DefaultEncoding",
      MainClass.defaultSettings.ImageEncoding));
```

## Providing web service properties

Before we can get the web service to work, we need to provide some properties. One is the SOAP namespace of the web service, which is the UPnP-service-type URN:

```
public override string Namespace
{
  get
  {
    return "urn:schemas-upnp-org:service:" +
      "DigitalSecurityCameraStillImage:1";
  }
}
```

We also need to provide the UPnP service identity:

```
public override string ServiceID
{
  get
  {
    return "urn:upnp-org:serviceId:" +
      "DigitalSecurityCameraStillImage";
  }
}
```

If we want to be able to test the web service using a test form, we must enable this feature to be accessed from remote machines:

```
public override bool CanShowTestFormOnRemoteComputers
{
  get
  {
    return true;
  }
}
```

## Adding service properties

To facilitate working with evented state variables, we will define the service properties that encapsulate these state variables and notify the possible subscribers when changes occur. By using these properties, we make sure the corresponding state variables work as expected throughout the application. We begin with the DefaultResolution state variable, remembering that the actual value lies in the static defaultSettings database object:

```
public LinkSpriteJpegColorCamera.ImageSize DefaultResolution
{
  get
  {
    return MainClass.defaultSettings.Resolution;
  }
  set
  {
    if(value != MainClass.defaultSettings.Resolution)
    {
      MainClass.defaultSettings.Resolution = value;
      MainClass.defaultSettings.UpdateIfModified ();
      this.NotifySubscribers ("DefaultResolution",
        MainClass.defaultSettings.Resolution.ToString ().Substring
        (1));
    }
  }
}
```

Similarly, we encapsulate the DefaultCompressionLevel and DefaultEncoding state variables in two other properties, implemented in the same manner.

## Adding actions

Adding the actions from the service definition available at http://upnp.org/specs/ha/UPnP-ha-StillImage-v1-Service.pdf is a very simple task once we get this far. They are implemented as normal web methods. Input parameters are specified as normal method parameters, and output parameters are defined using the out keyword. It's sufficient here to simply show the web method declarations:

```
public void GetDefaultEncoding(out string RetEncoding);
public void SetDefaultEncoding(string ReqEncoding);
public void GetAvailableEncodings(out string
  RetAvailableEncodings);
```

Similar methods are then implemented for the `DefaultCompressionLevel` and `DefaultResolution` state variables as well.

 To return a UPnP error from a web method, simply throw an exception of the type `UPnPException` instead of the normal `HttpException`. It is common for UPnP service descriptions to specify certain UPnP errors to be returned for certain conditions.

It is similarly a very easy task to add actions that provide the caller with URLs to our image (/camera) and web presentation (/html) resources, with appropriate query parameters. The web method declarations for the corresponding actions are as follows:

```
public void GetImageURL(HttpServerRequest Request,
   string ReqEncoding, string ReqCompression,
   string ReqResolution, out string RetImageURL);

public void GetDefaultImageURL(HttpServerRequest Request,
   out string RetImageURL);

public void GetImagePresentationURL(HttpServerRequest Request,
   string ReqEncoding, string ReqCompression,
   string ReqResolution, out string RetImagePresentationURL);

public void GetDefaultImagePresentationURL(HttpServerRequest
   Request, out string RetImagePresentationURL);
```

# Using our camera

Our camera project is now complete. It can be run and tested using a browser for the web interface and an application like Device Spy from UPnP Developer Tools. Here, we will present how you can use the device from another application, such as from our controller application.

## Setting up UPnP

As in our camera project, we need to create a UPnP interface towards the network. For this, we need an HTTP server and an SSDP client:

```
private static HttpServer upnpServer;
private static SsdpClient ssdpClient;
```

First, we set up the HTTP server in the similar way we set up the camera project:

```
upnpServer = new HttpServer (8080, 10, true, true, 1);
Log.Information ("UPnP Server receiving requests on port " +
  upnpServer.Port.ToString ());
```

We also set up the SSDP client likewise:

```
ssdpClient = new SsdpClient (upnpServer, 10,
  true, true, false, false, false, 30);
```

When the application closes, we need to dispose of these two objects too to make sure any threads are closed as well. Otherwise, the application will not close properly.

```
ssdpClient.Dispose ();
upnpServer.Dispose ();
```

## Discovering devices and services

In our controller application, we will listen to notifications from UPnP-compliant still image cameras instead of actively publishing interfaces of our own. The SSDP client maintains a list of found devices and interfaces for us. All we need to do is react to changes to this list. We do this by adding an event handler for the `OnUpdated` event, as follows:

```
ssdpClient.OnUpdated += NetworkUpdated;
```

In our `OnUpdated` event handler, we can examine the SSDP client, which contains a list of devices found in the network in the `Devices` property:

```
private static void NetworkUpdated (object Sender, EventArgs e)
{
   IUPnPDevice[] Devices = ssdpClient.Devices;
```

We can loop through all the devices found and their services to see whether we can find a still image camera service somewhere:

```
foreach (IUPnPDevice Device in Devices)
{
  foreach (IUPnPService Service in Device.Services)
  {
    if(Service.ServiceType == "urn:schemas-" + upnp-org:service:"
      + "DigitalSecurityCameraStillImage:1")
    {
```

## Subscribing to events

Subscribing to events once you have an UPnP service is easy. First, you need to construct a callback URL to a resource on the local machine that will receive the event; then, you simply call the `SubscribeToEvents()` method as follows:

```
int TimeoutSec = 5 * 60;
string Sid = Service.SubscribeToEvents (Callback, ref TimeoutSec);
```

You provide the callback URL and a timeout parameter that provides the service with a timeout interval in seconds, before which the subscription needs to be updated, or it will automatically expire. Note that the service might update the timeout interval if it chooses to do so. The `SubscribeToEvents` method returns a **subscription identity** (**SID**) that can be used when referring to a subscription in the future. To update an active subscription, to stop it from expiring, the following call has to be made before the timeout event occurs:

```
TimeoutSec = 5 * 60;
Service.UpdateSubscription (Sid, ref TimeoutSec);
```

## Receiving events

We have already mentioned that events from the camera are posted to a callback URL, provided when subscribing to events from the service. We can use the predefined web resource class `UPnPEvents` that is defined in the `Clayster.Library.Internet.UPnP` namespace. It handles the `POST` request and decodes the payload. We begin by defining such a static resource variable in our application:

```
private static UPnPEvents events;
```

We then create an instance, with the resource name `/events` in our case, and register it with our HTTP server dedicated to UPnP:

```
events = new UPnPEvents ("/events");
upnpServer.Register (events);
```

This resource has an event called `OnEventsReceived`, which is raised whenever an event is received. We add an event handler for this event:

```
events.OnEventsReceived += EventsReceived;
```

In our event handler, we can access any state variables provided in the event message by examining the `PropertySet` event argument property. Any part of the URL path trailing after `/events` will be available in the `SubItem` property:

```
private static void
   EventsReceived(object Sender,UPnPPropertySetEventArgs e)
{
   string SubPath = e.SubItem;
   Dictionary<string,string> Variables =
      new Dictionary<string,string>();

   foreach(KeyValuePair<string,string> Var in e.PropertySet)
      Variables [Var.Key] = Var.Value;
```

For a detailed description on how cameras are tracked in the network by the controller application and how event subscriptions are maintained, please refer to *Appendix N, Tracking Cameras*.

## Executing actions

Now that we know what cameras are available in the network and their state variables, we want to use them by taking pictures with them. To do this, we need to call an action on each still image camera service, for instance, the `GetDefaultImageURL` action, so we get a URL we can use to take a picture and download the image. Calling a UPnP action is simple. If the variable Service is a UPnP Service, meaning it implements the `IUPnPService` interface, we first get a reference to the action we need to call. Since we already know it supports the still image camera service interface, we simply get the `GetDefaultImageURL` action as follows:

```
UPnPAction GetDefaultImageURL = Service ["GetDefaultImageURL"];
```

To call an action, we provide input parameters in a `Variables` collection, with `Variables` being defined in `Clayster.Library.Math`. Output parameters will be available after the call in the same collection. In our case, we have no input parameters and one output parameter. We execute the action as follows:

```
Variables v = new Variables ();
GetDefaultImageURL.Execute (v);
string ImageURL = (string)v ["RetImageURL"];
```

Once you have the URL, it is simply a matter of downloading the image, which implicitly takes a new picture. *Appendix M, Sending Mail with Snapshots*, describes in more detail how this method is used to download images from all the available cameras in the network and send them embedded in an HTML-formatted mail to a preconfigured mail address.

We now have a complete system. The following screenshot is taken from a mail sent from the controller where we can see who it is that sneaks into our office at night and steals our resistors:

**Motion detected**

Motion has been detected while the light is turned off.

**Camera Photos**

# Summary

In this chapter, you had a brief introduction to UPnP and how it can be used in Internet of Things applications. Apart from using the request/response pattern and web services, you now how to discover devices in the local area network and how to subscribe to events to detect changes in device states. You have also learned how to document available services and methods in interoperable documents and how such documents can be used to develop solutions where parts are interchangeable.

In the next chapter, we will introduce the CoAP protocol and see how it reduces the complexity of the HTTP protocol to be better suited for resource-constrained devices and networks.

# 4
# The CoAP Protocol

As we have seen, HTTP is a tremendously popular protocol. In *Chapter 3*, *The UPnP Protocol*, we also saw the benefits of simplifying HTTP and using it over UDP instead of TCP. But for tiny resource-constrained devices that communicate over resource-constrained IP networks, HTTPU is not a practical option because it requires too many resources and too much bandwidth. This is especially the case when the underlying network limits the size of datagrams, which is the case when you use **IPv6 over Low power Wireless Personal Area Networks (6LoWPAN)**, a radio networking protocol based on the latest version of **Internet Protocol Version 6 (IPv6)**. **Constrained Application Protocol (CoAP)** is an attempt to solve this. In this chapter, we will show you how CoAP can be used in IoT by applying it to the sensor, actuator, and controller projects defined in the previous chapters.

In this chapter, you will learn the following:

- The basic operations available in CoAP
- How to publish CoAP resources
- How to subscribe to CoAP events
- How to use blocks to transport large content
- How to discover existing CoAP resources
- How to test CoAP resources

All of the source code presented in this book is available for download. The source code for this chapter and the next one can be downloaded from https://github.com/Clayster/Learning-IoT-CoAP.

# Making HTTP binary

The main difference between CoAP and HTTPU is that CoAP replaces the text headers used in HTTPU with more compact binary headers, and furthermore, it reduces the number of options available in the header. This makes it much easier to encode and parse CoAP messages. CoAP also reduces the set of methods that can be used; it allows you to have four methods: GET, POST, PUT, and DELETE. Also, in CoAP, method calls can be made using confirmable and nonconfirmable message services. When you receive a confirmable message, the receiver always returns an acknowledgement. The sender can, in turn, resend messages if an acknowledgement is not returned within the given time period. The number of response code has also been reduced to make implementation simpler. CoAP also broke away from the Internet Media Type scheme used in HTTP and other protocols and replaced this with a reduced set of Content-Formats, where each format is identified by a number instead of its corresponding Internet Media Type. A detailed list of the numbers assigned to different options, methods, status code, and Content-Formats used in CoAP can be found at http://www.iana.org/assignments/core-parameters/.

Apart from retaining the request/response capabilities of HTTP and a reduced set of methods and options, CoAP also provides a few new features. Like with HTTPU, CoAP supports multicasting. This can be used to detect devices or communicate through firewalls, as we saw in *Chapter 3, The UPnP Protocol*. CoAP also provides a set of useful extensions. One of these extensions provides a block transfer algorithm, which allows you to transfer larger amounts of data. (In constrained networks, large might be very small, compared to normal home or office IP networks.) Another extension allows you to have an event subscription and notification architecture where observable resources, which emit notifications when events occur, can be subscribed to. CoAP also supports encryption in the unicast case through the use of **Datagram Transport Layer Security (DTLS)**. The unencrypted version of CoAP is displayed in the following protocol stack diagram:

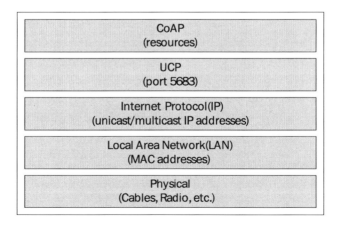

# Finding development tools

Since CoAP is relatively new, the availability of development tools for this protocol is somewhat restricted. There exists an add-on to Firefox, which allows you to view and interact with CoAP resources. This is called **Copper (Cu)** and can be downloaded from `https://addons.mozilla.org/en-US/firefox/addon/copper-270430/`. A web-based CoAP test tool can be found at `http://coap.me/`, and a CoAP interoperability server can be found at `http://vs0.inf.ethz.ch/`.

> Other useful information related to CoAP can be found at `http://coap.technology/`.

# Adding CoAP to our sensor

CoAP is a very lightweight protocol, and making our sensor interact with CoAP is very easy. First, we will set up a CoAP endpoint. (An endpoint acts both as a client and a server in the HTTP sense.). We can use the CoAP endpoint, `CoapEndpoint`, defined in the `Clayster.Library.Internet.CoAP` namespace. Before our main loop, we add the following:

```
CoapEndpoint CoapEndpoint = new CoapEndpoint ();
Log.Information ("CoAP endpoint receiving requests on port " +
  CoapEndpoint.Port.ToString ());
```

> If we want to see what communication is being established through CoAP endpoint, we would need to register a `LineListener` that would output everything to the console, as follows:
>
> ```
> CoapEndpoint.RegisterLineListener
>   (new ConsoleOutLineListenerSink
>     (BinaryFormat.Hexadecimal, true));
> ```
>
> There are many different types of line listeners available, defined in the `Clayster.Library.Internet.LineListeners` namespace; you can define your own line listeners by implementing the `ILineListener` interface.

## Defining our first CoAP resources

Our first CoAP resource will be called `temp/txt` and will publish the current temperature in plain text format. We do this as follows:

```
CoapEndpoint.RegisterResource ("temp/txt",
  "Current Temperature, as text.",
  CoapBlockSize.BlockLimit_64Bytes, false, 30, true,
  (Request, Payload) =>
  {
    return FieldNumeric.Format (temperatureC, "C", 1);
  });
```

While you can register any class derived from `CoapResource` as a resource on the CoAP endpoint, we prefer to use the lambda version that implicitly creates a resource for us since the actual resource code is so tiny. In the preceding code, the first parameter defines the name of the resource, in our case, `temp/txt`. If the IP address of our device is `192.168.0.29`, we will be able to access this resource through the use of the `coap://192.168.0.29/temp/txt` URL. The second parameter provides a descriptive title for the resource. This text will be used when documenting available resources on the end point, as will be described later. The third parameter is the default block size for the resource. When transmitting large payloads using CoAP, the payload will be divided into blocks if it is larger than the default block size. These blocks will then be transmitted to separate datagrams. The fourth parameter tells the endpoint that the resource does not handle any subpaths to the resource (`coap://192.168.0.29/temp/txt/example` for instance). We provide a default maximum age for the content returned by the resource in the fifth parameter; in our case, we set it to 30 seconds. In the sixth parameter, we tell the endpoint that the resource is observable. This means that subscribers can subscribe to events from this resource and the endpoint will regularly be notifying subscribers of new values. This will happen at least when the maximum age is reached or when the resource triggers a notification manually. Following these parameters, you can provide delegates for the GET, POST, PUT, and DELETE methods correspondingly. We only provide a GET method through a lambda function that returns a string containing the temperature formatted with one decimal and suffixed by a space and the unit C, for example, "23.1 C".

We define a light resource in the same way. Here, we create an observable `light/txt` resource that returns the light density in percent with a maximum age of 2 seconds:

```
CoapEndpoint.RegisterResource
  ("light/txt", "Current Light Density, as text.",
  CoapBlockSize.BlockLimit_64Bytes, false, 2, true,
  (Request, Payload) =>
```

```
{
    return FieldNumeric.Format (lightPercent, "%", 1);
});
```

# Manually triggering an event notification

The previous resources are observable, but they only notify event subscribers when the maximum age is reached. To be able to notify subscribers when something happens, you first need to have access to the CoAP resource. In our case, since these resources are created implicitly, we need to store the implicitly-generated resource. We create a static variable for the motion resource that will inform subscribers whether motion is detected:

```
private static CoapResource motionTxt = null;
```

We then register the motion resource, as we did with other resources, but we store the implicitly created resource object at the end:

```
motionTxt = CoapEndpoint.RegisterResource ("motion/txt",
  "Motion detection, as text.",CoapBlockSize.BlockLimit_64Bytes,
  false, 10, true,
  (Request, Payload) =>
  {
    return motionDetected ? "1" : "0";
  });
```

Here, our motion resource returns a plain text, either 1 or 0, depending on whether motion is detected or not. The resource is observable and updates subscribers with the current status of the motion detector at least every ten seconds. But we want to provide better response time than this without spamming the network. This can be done by manually triggering the event notification mechanism.

In our measurement loop, when we check the status of the PIR sensor, we check whether the state has changed. To notify any subscribers immediately if a change is detected, we simply call the NotifySubscribers() method, as follows:

```
if (MotionChanged && motionTxt != null)
  motionTxt.NotifySubscribers ();
```

# Registering data readout resources

Apart from the tiny momentary values published previously, we will also provide the XML, JSON, TURTLE, and RDF data formats through CoAP resources as well. Since these may be large, we must use the block transfer algorithm available in CoAP to divide the contents into multiple packets. This block transfer algorithm is incorporated into the CoAP endpoint class, and all we need to do is provide the desired block size (in bytes) when we register the resource. To make it easier to experiment, we will register our resources for all the available CoAP block sizes, which are defined in the `CoapBlockSize` enumeration. The available block sizes are 16, 32, 64, 128, 256, 512, and 1,024 bytes per block. The corresponding enumeration values are 0 for 16 bytes/block through 6 for 1024 bytes/block. We begin by looping through the available block sizes, avoiding the `BlockLimit_Datagram` option, which disables block transfer:

```
foreach (CoapBlockSize BlockSize in
  Enum.GetValues(typeof(CoapBlockSize)))
{
  if (BlockSize == CoapBlockSize.BlockLimit_Datagram)
    continue;

  string Bytes = (1 << (4 + (int)BlockSize)).ToString ();
```

We then register an XML resource for the corresponding block size:

```
CoapEndpoint.RegisterResource ("xml/" + Bytes,
  "Complete sensor readout, in XML. Control content using " +
  "query parmeters. Block size=" + Bytes + " bytes.",
  BlockSize, false, 30, false, CoapGetXml);
```

JSON, TURTLE, and RDF resources are registered in a similar manner. The only things that differ are the resource names, titles, and resource methods, as follows:

```
CoapEndpoint.RegisterResource ("json/" + Bytes,
  "Complete sensor readout, in JSON. Control content using " +
  "query parmeters. Block size=" + Bytes + " bytes.",
  BlockSize, false, 30, false, CoapGetJson);

CoapEndpoint.RegisterResource ("turtle/" + Bytes,
  "Complete sensor readout, in TURTLE. Control content " +
  "using query parmeters. Block size=" + Bytes + " bytes.",
  BlockSize, false, 30, false, CoapGetTurtle);

CoapEndpoint.RegisterResource ("rdf/" + Bytes,
  "Complete sensor readout, in RDF. Control content using " +
  "query parmeters. Block size=" + Bytes + " bytes.",
  BlockSize, false, 30, false, CoapGetRdf);
```

# Returning XML

To return XML from a CoAP resource method, you need to return an `XmlDocument` object. This way, `CoAPEndpoint` will know how to encode the response correctly. If you're returning a `string` value, it will be encoded as plain text, and not XML. We use our XML encoding methods defined earlier, load the XML into an `XmlDocument` object, and return it as follows:

```
private static object CoapGetXml (CoapRequest Request,
  object Payload)
{
  StringBuilder sb = new StringBuilder ();
  ISensorDataExport SensorDataExport =
    new SensorDataXmlExport (sb, false, true);
  ExportSensorData (SensorDataExport,
    new ReadoutRequest (Request.ToHttpRequest ()));

  XmlDocument Xml = new XmlDocument ();
  Xml.LoadXml (sb.ToString ());
  return Xml;
}
```

Note that the `ReadoutRequest` class that parses URL query options takes an `HttpServerRequest` object. This object contains the query parameters. We can use the `ToHttpRequest()` method on the `CoapRequest` object to convert the `CoAPRequest` object to a corresponding `HTTPRequest` object. Since CoAP is very similar to HTTP, we can reuse HTTP-based logic easily in this way.

At the time of writing this, there is no CoAP Content-Format for RDF. So we choose to return RDF data as XML data as well since it's the closest option:

```
private static object CoapGetRdf (CoapRequest Request,
  object Payload)
{
  StringBuilder sb = new StringBuilder ();
  HttpServerRequest HttpRequest = Request.ToHttpRequest ();
  ISensorDataExport SensorDataExport =
    new SensorDataRdfExport (sb, HttpRequest);
  ExportSensorData (SensorDataExport,
    new ReadoutRequest (HttpRequest));

  XmlDocument Xml = new XmlDocument ();
  Xml.LoadXml (sb.ToString ());
  return Xml;
}
```

## Returning JSON

To return JSON from a CoAP resource method, you need to return an array object if the result is an array, or `SortedDictionary<string,object>` if it is an object. These are classes that are recognized by the pluggable CoAP Content-Format encoders. In our case, we generate JSON using the methods developed earlier and use the `JsonUtilities` class to parse it and return the correct type of object:

```
private static object CoapGetJson (CoapRequest Request,
  object Payload)
{
  StringBuilder sb = new StringBuilder ();
  ISensorDataExport SensorDataExport =
    new SensorDataJsonExport (sb);
  ExportSensorData (SensorDataExport,
    new ReadoutRequest (Request.ToHttpRequest ()));
  return JsonUtilities.Parse (sb.ToString ());
}
```

## Returning plain text

As mentioned previously, returning plain text is done by simply returning a `string` value in the CoAP resource method. Since TURTLE does not have a CoAP Content-Format at the time of writing this, we return it as plain text instead. We use our previously defined method to generate TURTLE, as follows:

```
private static object CoapGetTurtle (CoapRequest Request,
  object Payload)
{
  StringBuilder sb = new StringBuilder ();
  HttpServerRequest HttpRequest = Request.ToHttpRequest ();
  ISensorDataExport SensorDataExport =
    new SensorDataTurtleExport (sb, HttpRequest);
  ExportSensorData (SensorDataExport,
    new ReadoutRequest (HttpRequest));
  return sb.ToString ();
}
```

Creating customized CoAP encoding and decoding is easy. All you need to do is implement one or both of the interfaces, `ICoapEncoder` and `ICoapDecoder` that are defined in `Clayster.Library.Internet.CoAP.Encoding`, in a custom class. There is no need to register the class anywhere. As long as the class has a public default constructor defined (one that takes no parameters), the framework will find it automatically.

## Discovering CoAP resources

The CoAP endpoint registers a resource by itself called `.well-known/core`. Here, it publishes a Link Format document called the **Constrained RESTful Environments (CoRE)** Link Format document. This document contains a list of resources published by the endpoint and some basic information about these documents. This document corresponds in some sense to WSDL documents for web services, even though the Link Format document is very lightweight. It consists of a sequence of resources and some corresponding attributes for each resource.

The generation of the Link Format document is done automatically. It includes resources, titles, and the observable status. If you want to include more information for a resource, you can override the `AppendLinkFormatResourceOptions` method in the `CoAPResource` class to add your own resource attributes to the document. The format of the document is fully described in RFC 6690, which you can read at `http://tools.ietf.org/html/rfc6690`.

When an entity wants to discover what resources are available on a device, it gets the link document from the `.well-known/core` resource. We can try this in the Cu Firefox plugin when our sensor has been started. By clicking on the **Discover** button, the interface downloads the document and populates a tree view to the left with the available resources that are found.

## Testing our CoAP resources

We can also select any of the resources found and try any of the methods in the interface. We can try to get the values of a resource by clicking on the **GET** button. The **Incoming** tab will display the results. If we want to observe how a resource varies over time, we need to click on the **Observe** button instead of the **GET** button. This also sends a GET query, but with observe options requesting to be notified when the resource is changed. If you send data to a resource, for instance by executing the POST or PUT method, you would need to provide the payload in the **Outgoing** tab. Any query parameters will be set in the URL as usual. The following image illustrates a GET operation against our TURTLE resource:

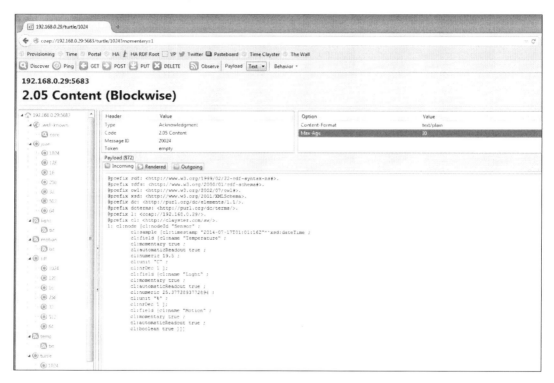

## Adding CoAP to our actuator

Adding CoAP to the actuator is done in more or less the same way as the sensor. The main difference between the two is that the resources will be used for the control resource instead of data readout. For this reason, the POST method will be used instead of GET to send data to the actuator. We start by adding a CoAP endpoint to our actuator, as follows:

```
CoapEndpoint CoapEndpoint = new CoapEndpoint ();
Log.Information ("CoAP endpoint receiving requests on port " +
  CoapEndpoint.Port.ToString ());
```

## Defining simple control resources

First, we define a series of simple control resources named doN/txt that can be used to read the state of the digital output, as well as change their status using simple plain text GET and POST method calls. In the resource name, N is used to identify which digital output is being referred to. When we register the resource, we need to provide two delegates. The first delegate will handle the GET method call and the second delegate will handle the POST method call. This can be seen in the following code snippet:

```
for(i = 1; i <= 8; i++)
{
  CoapEndpoint.RegisterResource("do" + i.ToString() + "/txt",
    "Digital Output " + i.ToString() + ", as text.",
    CoapBlockSize.BlockLimit_64Bytes, false, 30, false,
    CoapGetDigitalOutputTxt, CoapSetDigitalOutputTxt);
}
```

Similarly, we define a compound resource named do/txt that can be used to manage all the output in one operation:

```
CoapEndpoint.RegisterResource("do/txt",
  "Digital Outputs, as a number 0-255 as text.",
  CoapBlockSize.BlockLimit_64Bytes, false, 30, false,
  CoapGetDigitalOutputsTxt, CoapSetDigitalOutputsTxt);
```

We also publish a simple resource named alarm/txt for the alarm:

```
CoapEndpoint.RegisterResource("alarm/txt",
  "Alarm Output " + i.ToString () + ", as text.",
  CoapBlockSize.BlockLimit_64Bytes, false, 30, false,
  CoapGetAlarmOutputTxt, CoapSetAlarmOutputTxt);
```

 The source code for the actuator project also contains resources to provide the sensor data readout of the actuator. This is implemented in the same manner as for the sensor project.

# Parsing the URL in CoAP

The `CoapGetDigitlOutputTxt` method uses the URL to identify which digital output is being referenced. In CoAP, you don't need to parse the URL as a string since the request is not made in the form of a string URL to begin with. Instead, all parts of the URL are sent as options in the request. To start, let's first define our `GET` method that returns the current state of a digital output:

```
private static object CoapGetDigitalOutputTxt
  (CoapRequest Request, object DecodedPayload)
{
  int Index;

  if(!GetDigitalOutputIndex(Request, out Index))
    throw new CoapException
      (CoapResponseCode.ClientError_NotFound);
    return digitalOutputs [Index - 1].Value ? "1" : "0";
}
```

So, to find the digital output, we need to loop through the options of the CoAP request, single out the URI Path options (defined by the `CoapOptionUriPath` class, which is defined in the `Clayster.Library.Internet.CoAP.Options` namespace), and then extract the index from these options if found. Note that each segment in the path is represented by a `UriPath` option. So, the `do1/txt` resource is represented by two URI path options: one for `do1` and another for `txt`. This can be done as follows:

```
private static bool GetDigitalOutputIndex (CoapRequest Request,
  out int Index)
{
  CoapOptionUriPath Path;
  Index = 0;
  foreach (CoapOption Option in Request.Options)
  {
    if ((Path = Option as CoapOptionUriPath) != null &&
      Path.Value.StartsWith ("do"))
    {
      if (int.TryParse (Path.Value.Substring (2),
        out Index))
        return true;
    }
  }
  return false;
}
```

> Other useful options include the `CoapOptionAccept` option, where the client tells the server what type of content it desires, and the `CoapOptionUriQuery` option, where each similar option provides one query statement of the form p=v for a parameter p and a value v.

# Controlling the output using CoAP

The `CoapGetDigit1OutputTxt` method defined in the previous section returns a simple string containing 1 if the corresponding digital output is *high* and 0 if it is *low*. Let's now implement the POST method that will allow us to control the output using the text payload provided in the same format. We first define the method as follows:

```
private static object CoapSetDigitalOutputTxt
   (CoapRequest Request, object DecodedPayload)
{
  int Index;
  if(!GetDigitalOutputIndex (Request, out Index))
    throw new CoapException
      (CoapResponseCode.ClientError_NotFound);
```

Data posted along with the method call is found in the `DecodedPayload` parameter. What type of value this is depends on how the call was encoded. We first check whether it has been encoded as a plain text string:

```
string s = DecodedPayload as string;
```

If Content-Format information is left out of the call, the decoder wouldn't know how to decode the payload. In this case, the payload is simply an array of bytes. To improve interoperability, we will provide default decoding of such data by explicitly converting it into a string, as follows:

```
if(s == null && DecodedPayload is byte[])
  s = System.Text.Encoding.UTF8.GetString
    ((byte[])DecodedPayload);
```

Next, we have to parse the string. If not successful, we consider it a bad request and return a corresponding error to the caller:

```
bool b;
if(s == null || .XmlUtilities.TryParseBoolean (s, out b))
  throw new CoapException
    (CoapResponseCode.ClientError_BadRequest);
```

We then perform the actual control in the same manner as done in the case of HTTP. When done, we return a successful response code to the caller in the following manner:

```
  return CoapResponseCode.Success_Changed;
}
```

>  Notice that when returning content, you return the object itself. A CoAP encoder will be assigned that will encode the object for you. In this case, the response code of the message will automatically be set to `Success_Content`. If you don't want to return any content and only return a specific response code, you simply need to return a value of the `CoapResponseCode` enumeration type.

The other control methods are implemented in a similar manner and can be viewed in the source code for the *Actuator* project.

# Using CoAP in our controller

Like with the sensor and the actuator, we need a CoAP endpoint in our controller to be able to communicate over CoAP:

```
private static void MonitorCoap()
{
   CoapEndpoint Endpoint = new CoapEndpoint();
```

## Monitoring observable resources

We want to monitor two of our observable resources: the light sensor and the motion detector on our sensor. The simplest way to do this is to use the `CoapObserver` class, as shown in the next code snippet. This class performs the corresponding event subscription call to the resource and makes sure the values are constantly being reported, as expected. If no values are received within a given time frame, it will issue new event subscription calls. In this way, the observer recovers messages if they are lost or the observed resource is restarted:

```
CoapObserver LightObserver = new CoapObserver
   (Endpoint, true,"192.168.0.15", CoapEndpoint.DefaultCoapPort,
   "light/txt",string.Empty, 2 * 5);
CoapObserver MotionObserver = new CoapObserver
   (Endpoint, true, "192.168.0.15", CoapEndpoint.DefaultCoapPort,
   "motion/txt", string.Empty, 10 * 5);
```

The first parameter in the constructor refers to the CoAP endpoint that is responsible for the communication. The second Boolean parameter tells the observer whether *confirmable* or *nonconfirmable* messages are to be used. Confirmable messages require acknowledgment messages to be sent when received, which permits the sender to use a retry mechanism to make an attempt to ensure the message is delivered even in cases when messages are dropped for various reasons.

The third parameter is the IP address or the hostname of the machine hosting the observable resource. The fourth parameter is the corresponding CoAP port that is used. Following these parameters is the name of the resource. This is followed by any query parameters (none in our case) and eventually an acceptable number of seconds before new subscription requests could be sent, unless notifications are received within this time frame. As a window, we use five times the maximum age for our resources for when should the notifications be received or new subscription requests sent.

## Receiving notifications

There are two events in the observer class: `OnDataReceived` is raised when a new notification is received and `OnError` when an error message or timeout event occurs. These two events can be used to control the behavior of our application. We begin by declaring two local variables:

```
bool HasLightValue = false;
bool HasMotionValue = false;
```

We use the `OnDataReceived` event to react to incoming light density notifications, as follows:

```
LightObserver.OnDataReceived += (o, e) =>
{
```

The notification payload from the resource will be a string, and it is available in the `Response` property. We examine it and see whether it has the correct format and whether we can extract the numerical value from it:

```
string s = e.Response as string;
double d;

if(!string.IsNullOrEmpty(s) && s.EndsWith(" %") &&
  XmlUtilities.TryParseDouble(s.Substring(0, s.Length - 2),
  out d))
{
```

If we can do this, we store it in our control variables:

```
lightPercent = d;
if(!HasLightValue)
{
  HasLightValue = true;
  if(HasMotionValue)
    hasValues = true;
}
```

Having done this, we call the `CheckControlRules` method defined earlier. This method will look for the available values and signal appropriate actions:

```
        CheckControlRules();
    }
};
```

We implement the reception of motion notifications in a similar manner.

## Performing control actions

The last thing we need to do is perform the actual control actions by calling the resources defined in the actuator. Control actions in our application are flagged through event objects that the controller monitors. Instead of calling an HTTP resource, as we did previously to set the LEDs of the actuator corresponding to the value of the light sensor reports, we send a confirmable POST message using CoAP. Here, the variable `i` contains a value between 0 and 255 representing the state of each LED:

```
Endpoint.StartPOST(true, "192.168.0.23",
    CoapEndpoint.DefaultCoapPort, "do/txt", string.Empty,
    i.ToString(), CoapBlockSize.BlockLimit_64Bytes, null, null);
```

We use the asynchronous `StartPOST()` method instead of the synchronous `POST()` method since for our purposes, it is sufficient to start sending the command. Since we use the confirmable message service (the first parameter), the CoAP endpoint will perform retries if no acknowledgement is received from the actuator. The second and third parameters define the name or IP address of the host machine hosting the resource, together with the port number to use. The fourth parameter corresponds to the actual resource, and the fifth to any query parameters (none in our case). The sixth parameter contains the actual payload of the message, which in our case is simply the byte value that corresponds to the digital output states. After the payload, we define a maximum block size for the delivery of the message. Finally, a `callback` method is sent to call when the message has been sent or failed, and a state parameter is sent to the `callback` method. In our example, we don't need to worry about the success or failure of the message; so we leave these as null. Sending the command to control the alarm output is done in a similar manner.

We are now done with the CoAP implementation in the sensor, actuator, and controller applications. To access the complete source code, please download the example projects.

You are encouraged to compare the communication between the sensor, controller, and actuator using line listeners, WireShark, or other sniffing tools. You should do this using the HTTP versions from the previous chapter first and then the CoAP versions from this chapter. This will enable you to see the real differences between HTTP and CoAP and be able to compare telegram sizes and so on.

## Summary

In this chapter, we covered the basics of the CoAP protocol along with some of its strengths and weaknesses. We have seen how we can use it in our sensor, actuator, and controller projects as a simple means to create Internet of Things applications.

In the next chapter, we will introduce the publish/subscribe pattern and the use of message brokers as an alternative method of communication.

# 5
# The MQTT Protocol

One of the major problems we encountered when we looked at the HTTP, UPnP, and CoAP protocols is how to cross firewall boundaries. Firewalls not only block incoming connection attempts, but they also hide a home or office network behind a single IP address. Unless the firewall blocks outgoing connections, which it does only if explicitly configured to do so, we can cross firewall boundaries if all the endpoints in a conversation act as clients to a common message broker that lies outside of the firewall and is therefore accessible to everybody. The message broker acts as a server, but all it does is relay messages between clients. One protocol that uses message brokers is the **Message Queue Telemetry Transport** (**MQTT**) protocol.

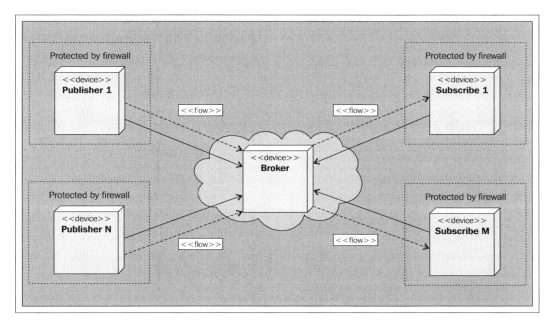

*The MQTT Protocol*

In this chapter, you will learn the following concepts:

- The basic operations available in MQTT
- How to publish data using MQTT topics
- How to subscribe to MQTT topics
- How to implement MQTT in the sensor, actuator, and controller

 All of the source code presented in this book is available for download. The source code for this chapter and the next one can be downloaded from `https://github.com/Clayster/Learning-IoT-MQTT`

# Publishing and subscribing

The MQTT protocol is based on the publish/subscribe pattern, as opposed to the request/response and the event subscription patterns studied in the previous chapters. The publish/subscribe pattern has three types of actors:

- **Publisher**: The role of the publisher is to connect to the message broker and publish content
- **Subscriber**: They connect to the same message broker and subscribe to content that they are interested in
- **Message broker**: This makes sure that the published content is relayed to interested subscribers

Content is identified by topic. When publishing content, the publisher can choose whether the content should be retained by the server or not. If retained, each subscriber will receive the latest published value directly when subscribing. Furthermore, topics are ordered into a tree structure of topics, much like a filesystem. The forward slash character (/) is used as a delimiter when describing a topic path. When subscribing to content, a subscriber can subscribe to either a specific topic by providing its path, or an entire branch using the hash wildcard character (#). There's also a single-level wildcard character: the plus character (+). As an example, to illustrate topic semantics, our sensor will publish measured temperature on the `Clayster/LearningIoT/Sensor/Temperature` topic. Subscribing to `Clayster/+/Sensor/#` will subscribe to all the subbranches of the `Sensor` class that start with `Clayster/`, then any subtopic, which in turn will have a `Sensor/` subtopic.

The architecture of MQTT is shown in the following diagram:

| MQTT (topics) | MQTT over SSL/TLS (topics) |
|---|---|
| TCP (port 1883) | TCP (port 8883) |
| Internet Protocol(IP) (unicase/muticast IP addresses) ||
| Local Area Network(LAN) (MAC addresses) ||
| Physical (Cables, Radio, etc.) ||

There are three Quality of Service levels in MQTT available while publishing content. The lowest level is an unacknowledged service. Here, the message is delivered at most once to each subscriber. The next level is an acknowledged service. Here, each recipient acknowledges the receipt of the published information. If no receipt is received, the information can be sent again. This makes sure the information is delivered at least once. The highest level is called the assured service. Here, information is not only acknowledged but sent in two steps. First it is transmitted and then delivered. Each step is acknowledged. This makes it possible to make sure that the content is delivered exactly once to each subscriber.

> The support for user authentication in MQTT is weak. Plain text username and password authentication exists, but it provides an obvious risk if the server is not hosted in a controlled environment. To circumvent the most obvious problems, MQTT can be used over an encrypted connection using SSL/TLS. In this case, it is important for clients to validate server certificates else user credentials may be compromised.
>
> Other methods, not defined in the MQTT protocol itself, include the use of client-side certificates or preshared keys to identify clients, instead of using the username and password option provided by the protocol. Proprietary methods of encrypting the contents can also be used to make sure only receivers with sufficient credentials can decrypt the contents. Even though this method works, it reduces interoperability and provides an additional load on each device, which is contrary to the stated goal of the protocol.
>
> As the MQTT protocol itself does not consider security, it is very important for developers to consider security themselves. Furthermore, user credentials must be managed manually or by using proprietary out-of-band methods.

# Adding MQTT support to the sensor

To add MQTT support to our sensor, we will use the `MqttClient` class defined in the `Clayster.Library.Internet.MQTT` namespace. We start by adding the following namespace to our `using` section in the code:

```
using Clayster.Library.Internet.MQTT;
```

Communication with the MQTT server will be done from a separate thread in our example. This is to assure that we avoid timing problems with the measurement logic. When new values are available, we flag this fact to the MQTT thread using auto-reset event objects. So, we need the following static variables:

```
private static Thread mqttThread = null;
private static AutoResetEvent mqttNewTemp =
  new AutoResetEvent(false);
private static AutoResetEvent mqttNewLight =
  new AutoResetEvent(false);
private static AutoResetEvent mqttNewMotion =
  new AutoResetEvent(false);
```

The application will then publish values to MQTT topics if a significant change has occurred, or when the given time has passed since its last publication. So, we can create variables for the last published value as well as the time when the last publication occurred.

```
private static double mqttLastTemp = 0;
private static double mqttLastLight = 0;
private static bool mqttLastMotion = false;
private static DateTime mqttLastTempPublished = DateTime.MinValue;
private static DateTime mqttLastLightPublished =
  DateTime.MinValue;
private static DateTime mqttLastMotionPublished =
  DateTime.MinValue;
```

# Controlling the thread life cycle

Before the main loop, we start the MQTT thread in the usual manner, making sure to set the thread priority to `BelowNormal` so that it does not affect the way it is normally executed:

```
mqttThread = new Thread (MqttThread);
mqttThread.Name = "MQTT";
mqttThread.Priority = ThreadPriority.BelowNormal;
mqttThread.Start();
```

>  We create our thread using the thread priority just below the normal (`BelowNormal`) priority. This means the thread will not interfere with normal operation in case the device CPU usage reaches 100 percent. When CPU usage is below 100 percent, this thread will work as a normal thread. Since communication is normally dropped when this happens, this does not imply loss of real functionality.

When we close the application, we must also make sure the thread is closed properly. We use the `Abort()` method on the thread to accomplish this:

```
if(mqttThread != null)
{
  mqttThread.Abort ();
  mqttThread = null;
}
```

## Flagging significant events

In the `SampleSensorValues()` method where we sample new sensor values, we need to detect significant events that the MQTT thread needs to react to. We can start with the motion detector. After it notifies any CoAP subscribers, we also need to signal the MQTT thread that the Boolean value has changed:

```
if (MotionChanged)
{
  if (motionTxt .= null)
    motionTxt.NotifySubscribers ();

  mqttNewMotion.Set ();
  mqttLastMotionPublished = Now;
  mqttLastMotion = motionDetected;
```

However, we also need to republish the value if it has been a long time since a value was published, which can be done with the following code:

```
}
else if((Now - mqttLastMotionPublished).TotalMinutes >= 10)
{
  mqttNewMotion.Set ();
  mqttLastMotionPublished = Now;
  mqttLastMotion = motionDetected;
}
```

Significant events for Boolean values are easy to define. But what is a significant event for a numerical value? In our implementation, a significant event is if the temperature change is more than half a degree centigrade or if more than ten minutes has passed. Here, what constitutes the word "significant" depends on what type of temperature we are measuring. This limit could be configurable if the context is not clear.

In the same way, we define a significant event for the light sensor as a change in one unit of a percent or ten minutes since it was last published, whichever comes first:

```
if ((Now - mqttLastLightPublished).TotalMinutes >= 10 ||
  System.Math.Abs (lightPercent - mqttLastLight) >= 1.0)
{
  mqttNewLight.Set ();
  mqttLastLightPublished = Now;
  mqttLastLight = lightPercent;
}
```

Since the request/response pattern is difficult to implement using MQTT (you would have to invent separate topics to send requests on), you need a method to notify subscribers of the current status of the sensor as well as tell them that you are alive and well. One way to accomplish this is to, with some regularity, publish the current status, even if the change from the last published value is not great or doesn't exist at all.

## Connecting to the MQTT server

From our communication thread, we use the `MqttClient` class to communicate with the MQTT server:

```
MqttClient Client = null;
```

In the following example, we will use a publicly available MQTT server hosted by `eclipse.org`. It allows anybody to connect and publish information, so we simply provide a username for appearance's sake and leave the password empty. The last Boolean parameter specifies whether we want to use SSL/TLS encryption or not. In our case, we will not bother with encryption of the connection since the data will be publicly available on the Internet anyway:

```
if (Client == null)
{
  Client = new MqttClient ("iot.eclipse.org",
    MqttClient.DefaultPort, "LearningIoTSensor", string.Empty,
    false);
```

>  If you want to follow the communication, you can register a `LineListener` with the MQTT client object as follows:
> ```
> Client.RegisterLineListener (
>     new ConsoleOutLineListenerSink (
>         BinaryFormat.Hexadecimal));
> ```

We then open the connection and log in to the server. In the CONNECT() method, you need to specify the keepalive time in seconds and whether the connection is a clean connection or not. A clean connection discards any pending notifications stored on the server. If you wish to reconnect to the server, you can choose not to use a clean connection. The server will then send you any notifications it has stored in the session, while you were not connected, if the session has not been timed out and removed.

```
Client.Open ();
Client.CONNECT (20, true);
```

Finally, it's a good idea to log an event in the event log indicating that the MQTT connection is active:

```
Log.Information ("Publishing via MQTT to " +
    "Clayster/LearningIoT/Sensor @ ", EventLevel.Minor,
    Client.Host + ":" + Client.PortNumber.ToString ());
}
```

>  You can install and host your own MQTT message brokers if you want to. You can find several of these to choose from via https://github.com/mqtt/mqtt.github.io/wiki/servers.

## Publishing the content

The application flags significant events to consider using event objects. So we first need to create an array of the available events to monitor:

```
WaitHandle[] Events = new WaitHandle[]
{
    mqttNewTemp, mqttNewLight, mqttNewMotion
};
```

In our infinite loop, we then wait for any of the events to occur:

```
switch (WaitHandle.WaitAny (Events, 1000))
{
}
```

We begin by publishing temperature information, if such an event is detected. Here we publish the current temperature using the acknowledged message service as a string with one decimal, suffixed by a space and the unit C:

```
case 0:// New temperature
  Client.PUBLISH("Clayster/LearningIoT/Sensor/Temperature",
    FieldNumeric.Format (temperatureC, "C", 1),
    MqttQoS.QoS1_Acknowledged, true);
  break;
```

MQTT is a binary protocol, and it does not support the encoding or decoding of content. We must keep track of encoding and decoding ourselves. The `MqttClient` library provides you with a `PUBLISH()` method that allows you to publish binary content. It also has overrides that allow you to publish text and XML content using simple UTF-8 encoding.

Similarly, we will publish the current light density as a string with one decimal suffixed by a space and a percent character (%):

```
case 1:// New light
  Client.PUBLISH ("Clayster/LearningIoT/Sensor/Light",
    FieldNumeric.Format (lightPercent, "%", 1),
    MqttQoS.QoS1_Acknowledged, true);
  break;
```

The motion detector only contains a Boolean value. We publish this value as either a string containing the digit 1 if motion is detected or 0 if not.

```
case 2:// New motion
  Client.PUBLISH ("Clayster/LearningIoT/Sensor/Motion",
    motionDetected ? "1" : "0", MqttQoS.QoS1_Acknowledged, true);
  break;
```

One of the strengths of MQTT is that it allows you to send large amounts of data to one topic in one message. The size limit for topic content in MQTT is 256 megabytes. This makes it possible to post multimedia content without having to break up the content into segments or use streaming.

# Adding MQTT support to the actuator

The actuator will act as a subscriber in the MQTT network by subscribing to the commands published on specific command topics. Before we enter the main loop, we create an MQTT client connection in the same way we did for the sensor:

```
MqttClient MqttClient = new MqttClient("iot.eclipse.org",
  MqttClient.DefaultPort,"LearningIoTActuator", string.Empty,
  false);
MqttClient.Open();
MqttClient.CONNECT(20, true);
```

## Initializing the topic content

We can take advantage of this opportunity to also publish the current (or saved) states of the actuator output to the topics we will soon subscribe to. This is to make sure that the output and topic contents are consistent. Let's have a look at the following code:

```
MqttClient.PUBLISH("Clayster/LearningIoT/Actuator/ao",
  state.Alarm ? "1" : "0", MqttQoS.QoS1_Acknowledged, true);
MqttClient.PUBLISH("Clayster/LearningIoT/Actuator/do",
  wsApi.GetDigitalOutputs().ToString(),
  MqttQoS.QoS1_Acknowledged, true);

for (i = 1; i <= 8; i++)
  MqttClient.PUBLISH
    ("Clayster/LearningIoT/Actuator/do" + i.ToString (),
    wsApi.GetDigitalOutput (i) ? "1" : "0",
    MqttQoS.QoS1_Acknowledged, true);
```

Here we publish a subtopic named `ao` to control the analog output, subtopics from `do1` to `do8` for individual digital output, and a compound subtopic named `do` that can be used to control all the eight digital output in one go.

## Subscribing to topics

Subscribing to events in MQTT is simple. You just call the SUBSCRIBE() method with the set of topics (including wildcards) you are interested in, together with their corresponding Quality of Service level, by providing the quality of service level you wish to support. In our case, we only subscribe to one branch in the topic tree:

```
MqttClient.SUBSCRIBE (new KeyValuePair<string, MqttQoS>
  ("Clayster/LearningIoT/Actuator/#",MqttQoS.QoS1_Acknowledged));
```

[  To unsubscribe from topics currently subscribed to, you simply need to call the `UNSUBSCRIBE()` method, providing the set of topics to unsubscribe. ]

Whenever data is published to any topic in the `Clayster/LearningIoT/Actuator/` branch, the `OnDataPublished` event on the MQTT client object will be raised. We add an event handler for the event as follows:

```
MqttClient.OnDataPublished += OnMqttDataPublished;
```

We also make sure to log an informative event stating that the actuator will now receive commands over MQTT:

```
Log.Information ("Receiving commands via MQTT from " +
  "Clayster/LearningIoT/Actuator @ ", EventLevel.Minor,
  MqttClient.Host + ":" + MqttClient.PortNumber.ToString ());
```

[  Make sure to add the event handler before you subscribe to the topics; otherwise, you might lose the retained information the broker sends you immediately upon subscribing. ]

## Receiving the published content

The event arguments of our event contain both the topic and binary data for all of the content that is published to a topic we have subscribed to. We must handle the decoding of content ourselves, but since we only accept string content, we can begin our event handler as follows:

```
private static void OnMqttDataPublished (object Sender,
  DataPublishedEventArgs e)
{
  string Topic = e.Topic;
  if (!Topic.StartsWith ("Clayster/LearningIoT/Actuator/"))
    return;
  string s = System.Text.Encoding.UTF8.GetString (e.Data);
  Topic = Topic.Substring (30);
  switch (Topic)
  {
    // Topic data to be processed here.
  }
}
```

When you enter the `switch` statement, you'll find that the `Topic` variable contains the name of the subtopic with the new published value and the `s` string contains the actual string value.

# Decoding and parsing content

Handling incoming content is now straightforward. Since we cannot check from where a command is issued, unless it is encoded into the content payload, we must always make sure to check that the content published is correctly formatted and we discard erroneous publications. The handling of the do subtopic, which controls all the eight digital outputs in one go, is done as follows:

```
case "do":
  int IntValue;
  if(int.TryParse(s, out IntValue) && IntValue >= 0 &&
    IntValue <= 255)
  {
    int i;
    bool b;
    for(i = 0; i < 8; i++)
    {
      b = (IntValue & 1) != 0;
      digitalOutputs [i].Value = b;
      state.SetDO(i, b);
      IntValue >>= 1;
    }
    state.UpdateIfModified();
  }
  break;
```

Controlling the Boolean alarm output is implemented in a similar manner:

```
case "ao":
  bool BoolValue;
  if(XmlUtilities.TryParseBoolean(s, out BoolValue))
  {
    if(BoolValue)
    {
      AlarmOn();
      state.Alarm = true;
    }
    else
    {
      AlarmOff();
      state.Alarm = false;
    }
    state.UpdateIfModified();
  }
  break;
```

Individual digital output is controlled by different topics. To set it correctly, we need to parse both the topic and content properly, as follows:

```
default:
  if (Topic.StartsWith("do") &&
    int.TryParse(Topic.Substring(2), out IntValue) &&
    IntValue >= 1 && IntValue <= 8 &&
    XmlUtilities.TryParseBoolean(s, out BoolValue))
  {
    digitalOutputs [IntValue - 1].Value = BoolValue;
    state.SetDO(IntValue - 1, BoolValue);
    state.UpdateIfModified();
  }
  break;
```

# Adding MQTT support to the controller

As you have seen, all endpoints in MQTT connect to the broker in the same way as MQTT clients. The same is true for the controller, which subscribes to the information published by the sensor and publishes commands to the actuator, as shown in the following code:

```
Client = new MqttClient ("iot.eclipse.org",
  MqttClient.DefaultPort,"LearningIoTController",
  string.Empty, false);
Client.Open ();
Client.CONNECT (20, true);
```

# Handling events from the sensor

To handle events from the sensor, we need to register an event handler, as we did for the actuator; this time, we will register it as a lambda function for the sake of simplicity. This means we will provide the code to handle events before we could actually perform the subscription.

```
Client.OnDataPublished += (Sender, e) =>
{
  string Topic = e.Topic;
  if(!Topic.StartsWith ("Clayster/LearningIoT/Sensor/"))
  return;

  string s = System.Text.Encoding.UTF8.GetString(e.Data);
  PhysicalMagnitude Magnitude;
  bool b;
  Topic = Topic.Substring(28);
```

```
switch(Topic)
{
  // Topic data to be processed here.
}
};
```

## Decoding and parsing sensor values

When a new light value is reported, we make sure to parse it and flag the event, as we have done previously for other protocols. We use the `PhysicalMagnitude` class defined in `Clayster.Library.Math` to help us parse a numerical value suffixed by a physical unit:

```
case "Light":
  if(PhysicalMagnitude.TryParse (s, out Magnitude) &&
      Magnitude.Unit == "%" && Magnitude.Value >= 0 &&
      Magnitude.Value <= 100)
  {
    lightPercent = Magnitude.Value;
    if(!HasLightValue)
    {
      HasLightValue = true;
      if(HasMotionValue)
        hasValues = true;
    }
    CheckControlRules();
  }
  break;
```

In a similar manner, we parse incoming changes reported by the motion detector and report it to the underlying control logic:

```
case "Motion":
  if(!string.IsNullOrEmpty(s) &&
      XmlUtilities.TryParseBoolean(s, out b))
  {
    motion = b;
    if(!HasMotionValue)
    {
      HasMotionValue = true;
      if(HasLightValue)
        hasValues = true;
    }
    CheckControlRules();
  }
  break;
```

## Subscribing to sensor events

We can now subscribe to the events published by the sensor similar to the way the actuator subscribed to control commands:

```
Client.SUBSCRIBE(new KeyValuePair<string, MqttQoS>
  ("Clayster/LearningIoT/Sensor/#", MqttQoS.QoS1_Acknowledged));
Log.Information("Listening on MQTT topic " +
  "Clayster/LearningIoT/Sensor @ ", EventLevel.Minor,Client.Host +
  ":" + Client.PortNumber.ToString());
```

## Controlling the actuator

Now that we have received sensor data and calculated the desired control actions, all the controller needs to do is publish the corresponding control commands on the topics listened to by the actuator. To highlight the fact that we use binary data in MQTT and control encoding and decoding ourselves, we will first define a UTF-8 encoder that will encode strings to a binary format without using a byte order mark or preamble:

```
UTF8Encoding Encoder = new UTF8Encoding (false);
```

## Controlling the LED output

The final step is to publish commands as they occur by encoding the corresponding command strings and publishing them on the corresponding command topics. We begin by the command to update the LEDs of the actuator:

```
switch(WaitHandle.WaitAny(Handles, 1000))
{
  case 0:// Update LEDS
    int i;
    lock(synchObject)
    {
      i = lastLedMask;
    }
    Client.PUBLISH("Clayster/LearningIoT/Actuator/do",
      Encoder.GetBytes(i.ToString ()),
      MqttQoS.QoS1_Acknowledged, true);
```

Even though it is not needed for our immediate control needs, we will also publish individual control commands. Since content is retained by the message broker, content on the topics will be consistent if the actuator reboots and receives the latest control commands from the broker. Since the subtopics do1 to do8 correspond to the bits of the compound subtopic do, we simply loop through the bits in do and publish each one to its corresponding subtopic. This is performed with the following code:

```
for (int j = 1; j <= 8; j++)
{
   Client.PUBLISH("Clayster/LearningIoT/Actuator/do" +
     j.ToString (), Encoder.GetBytes ((i & 1).ToString ()),
     MqttQoS.QoS1_Acknowledged, true);
   i >>= 1;
}
break;
```

## Controlling the alarm output

We control the alarm output in the same way as we control the LED output. We wait for the event and publish the corresponding control command on the corresponding control topic:

```
case 1:// Update Alarm
   bool b;
   lock(synchObject)
   {
     b = lastAlarm.Value;
   }
   Client.PUBLISH("Clayster/LearningIoT/Actuator/ao",
     Encoder.GetBytes (b ? "1" : "0"),
     MqttQoS.QoS1_Acknowledged, true);
```

After we publish the control command, we also need to start the SendAlarmMail thread if the alarm is activated:

```
if(b)
{
   Thread T = new Thread (SendAlarmMail);
   T.Priority = ThreadPriority.BelowNormal;
   T.Name = "SendAlarmMail";
   T.Start ();
}
break;
```

# The MQTT Protocol

Finally, we must not forget to update any camera subscriptions we maintain on the UPnP network:

```
   default:// Timeout
      CheckSubscriptions (30);
      break;
}
```

Our controller is now ready to operate, together with the sensor and the actuator using MQTT as the control protocol. This means that all the three can reside in separate networks protected by individual firewalls. The only restriction to network topology we have is that any cameras used by the controller need to be in the same local area network as the controller itself.

If we have access to a tool that can be used to visualize MQTT topics, we can monitor how our devices operate. You can find many tools and applications for this purpose at `https://github.com/mqtt/mqtt.github.io/wiki/tools`.

In the following example, visualized by Clayster Management Tool, each topic in the topic tree is visualized as a node. Even if it cannot be seen in the print version of the book, the topics that publish Boolean properties are colored red and green depending on whether 1 or 0 is published. The numerical topics related to the light are colored from black to white, depending on how much light is reported. The temperature on the other hand is colored blue if cold (15 degree Celsius). If warmer, it is blended to green (about 20 degree Celsius) and finally blended to red if hot (25 degree Celsius). Colors here assume it is an in-door temperature we are measuring. A colored version of the image is available for download at the Packt Publishing website.

The topic tree is shown in the following screenshot:

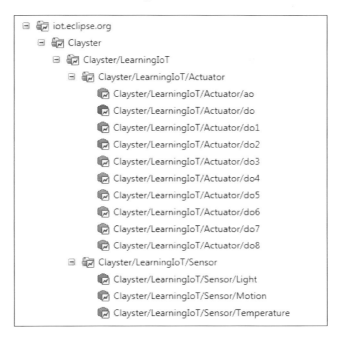

# Summary

In this chapter, we covered the basics of the MQTT protocol and some of its strengths and weaknesses. We have seen how we can use it in our sensor, actuator, and controller projects as a simple means to cross firewall boundaries.

In the next chapter, we will introduce the XMPP protocol and some of the new communication patterns it allows such as federation, global identity, presence, friendship, authorization, delegation of trust, provisioning, and so on. We will also show how these patterns can help us build a secure architecture for Internet of Things.

# The XMPP Protocol

In the previous chapter, we saw the benefits of using message brokers to cross firewall boundaries. But the MQTT protocol is limited to a single communication pattern: the publish/subscribe pattern. This is useful in cases where a thing only publishes data and has many consumers of its data, and where data is homogenous and most reported data items are actually used. If individually tailored messages, momentary values, or real-time or bidirectional communication is important, or if data is seldom used compared to the frequency with which it is updated, other communication patterns would be more appropriate.

In this chapter, we will introduce the **Extensible Messaging and Presence Protocol** (**XMPP**) protocol. The XMPP protocol also uses message brokers to bypass firewall barriers. But apart from the publish/subscribe pattern, it also supports other communication patterns, such as point-to-point request/response and asynchronous messaging, that allow you to have a richer communication experience. You will learn about:

- The basic operations available in XMPP
- How to add XMPP support to a generic device
- How to use provisioning to add an extra layer of security for your device
- How to communicate between our devices using XMPP
- How to configure your network using the provisioning server

> All the source code presented in this book is available for download. The source code for this chapter and the next can be downloaded from `https://github.com/Clayster/Learning-IoT-XMPP`

# XMPP basics

XMPP was originally designed for use in instant messaging applications (or chat). It is an open protocol, standardized by **Internet Engineering Task Force (IETF)**, as are HTTP and CoAP. Even though it was first designed for chat applications, it lends itself very well to other applications, such as the ones for IoT, due to its flexibility and richness of communication patterns. Before we start using XMPP in our projects, it might be a good idea to have a quick overview of what XMPP is.

# Federating for global scalability

The XMPP architecture builds on the tremendous success and global scalability of the **Simple Mail Transfer Protocol** (**SMTP**). The difference is that XMPP is designed for real-time instantaneous messaging applications, where smaller messages are sent with as little latency as possible and without any persistence.

XMPP uses a federated network of XMPP servers as message brokers to allow clients behind separate firewalls to communicate with each other. Each server controls its own domain and authenticates users on that domain. Clients can communicate with clients on other domains through the use of federation where the servers create connections between themselves in a secure manner to interchange messages between their domains. It is this federation that allows you to have a globally scalable architecture. All of this happens at the server level, so there is nothing that clients need to worry about. They only need to ensure that they maintain the connection with their respective servers, and through the servers, each of them will have the possibility to send messages to any other client in the federated network. It is this architecture of federation that makes XMPP scalable and allows you to make billions of devices communicate with each other in the same federated network.

The following illustration shows how clients (**C1**, **C2**, and **C3**) behind firewalls connect to different servers (**S1**, **S2**, and **S3**) in a federated network to exchange messages:

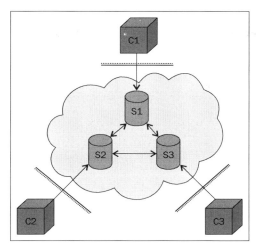

A small federated XMPP network

## Providing a global identity

XMPP servers do more than relay messages between clients. They also provide each client with an authenticated identity. If the server is a public server in the global federated network of XMPP servers, it is a global identity. When clients connect, the servers make sure the clients authenticate themselves by providing their corresponding client credentials, which would consist of a username and password. This authentication is done securely using an extensible architecture based on **Simple Authentication and Security Layer** (**SASL**). The connection can also be switched over to **Transport Layer Security** (**TLS**) through negotiation between the client and the server, encrypting the communication between them. The identity of the client is often called XMPP address or **Jabber ID** (**JID**).

>  The XMPP protocol was developed in a project named *Jabber*. For this reason, many terminologies retain this name.

Each connection is also bound to a specific resource, which is normally a random string. Together, the username, domain name, and resource constitute the full JID of a connection, while only the username and domain name constitute the bare JID of an account.

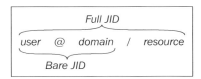

# Authorizing communication

Another important reason for using XMPP servers to relay communication instead of serverless peer-to-peer technologies is to assure the clients that only authorized communication will be relayed. This feature comes in handy, especially for small devices with limited decision-making capabilities. The server does so by ensuring that the full `JID` identifier instead of only the bare `JID` identifier is used to communicate with the application or device behind it. The reason is twofold:

- First, multiple clients might use the same account at the same time. You need to provide the resource part of the full `JID` for the XMPP Server to be able to determine which connection the corresponding message should be forwarded to. Only this connection will receive the message. This enables the actual clients to have direct communication between them.

- Second, only trusted parties (or friends) are given access to the resource part once the thing or application is connected. This means that, in turn, only friends can send messages between each other, as long as the resource parts are sufficiently long and random so they cannot be guessed and the resource part is kept hidden and not published somewhere else.

# Sensing online presence

To learn about the resource part of a corresponding client, you send a presence subscription to its bare `JID`. If accepted by the remote client, you will receive presence messages every time the state of the contact is changed, informing you whether it is online, offline, away, busy, and so on. In this presence message, you will also receive the full `JID` of the contact. Once a presence subscription has been accepted by the remote device, it might send you a presence subscription of its own, which you can either accept or reject. If both the parties accept it and subscribe to the presence from each other, then parties are said to be friends.

> In XMPP, there might be multiple clients that use the same bare `JID`. In solutions where this is the case, you would need to keep track of all the full `JID`s reported to you for each bare `JID`. But for all the examples in this book, we assume that each thing has its own `JID` and that only the corresponding thing will use its `JID`.
>
> If you, during development time, use another client to connect to an account used by a live thing, you might confuse it with its friends as your connection will send presence messages to all these friends. They might therefore direct the communication to the last application that was connected. When this application is closed down, you will need to reset, reconnect, or reset the presence status in the corresponding thing for its friends to be updated of the correct full `JID` to communicate with.

XMPP servers maintain lists of contacts for each account and their corresponding presence subscription statuses. These lists are called **rosters**. The client only needs to connect and then receive its roster from the server. This makes it possible to move the application between physical platforms and unnecessary to store contact information in the physical device.

## Using XML

XMPP communication consists of bidirectional streams of XML fragments. The reason for using XML has been debated since it affects message sizes negatively when compared to binary alternatives, but it has many positive implications as well. These can be listed as follows:

- Having a fixed content format makes the interchange and reuse of data simpler
- XML is simple to encode, decode, and parse, making data telegrams well-defined
- Using a text format makes telegrams readable by humans, which makes documentation and debugging simpler
- XML has standard tools for searching validation and transformation, which permits advanced operations and analysis to be performed on data without previous knowledge about message formats
- Through the use of XML namespaces, messages can be separated between protocol extensions and versioning is supported

> In cases where the message size is important, there are methods in XMPP that help compress XML to very efficient binary messages using **Efficient XML Interchange (EXI)**.

## Communication patterns

XMPP supports a rich set of communication patterns. It does this by providing three communication primitives called stanzas. We've already presented the first of these, the presence stanza. This is used to send information about oneself to interested and authorized parties. The second is the message stanza. This is used to send asynchronous messages to a given receiver. The third is the iq stanza, short for information/query. This stanza is used to provide a request/response communication pattern. A request is sent to a given receiver, which returns a response or an error, as appropriate.

There are four different kinds of receivers of stanzas. First, you have the peer. To communicate with a peer, you provide the full JID of the peer connection as the destination address of your stanza. Then you have a server. To communicate with a server directly, you use the domain name of the server as the destination address. A server might host server components of various kinds. These might be internal or external components hosted by external applications. These components are addressed using a corresponding subdomain name and can be dynamically discovered using simple requests to the server. Finally, you have a contact. To communicate with a contact, which is implicitly handled by your server and the server handling the contact, depending on the type of message, you need to use the base JID of the contact as the address.

Further communication patterns are provided by different server components hosted by the XMPP servers. Examples of such patterns include the publish/subscribe pattern, where data items are propagated to the subscribers, and the multicast pattern (in XMPP, this is called the multiuser chat), where messages are propagated to the members of a room in real time.

# Extending XMPP

So, through the use of XML, XMPP provides a protocol that is open, easy to use, extensible, and flexible. This has led to a series of extensions being created. Anybody can create proprietary extensions to XMPP, but there exists an open forum called **XMPP Standards Foundation** (**XSF**) that publishes a set of extensions which are openly reviewed and discussed within the forum and free for anybody to use. These extensions are called **XMPP Extension Protocols** (**XEPs**). XSF publishes such extensions to promote interoperability. Anybody can apply to become a member and thus work to promote the development of new or existing extensions.

XSF manages lists of extensions, the available server and client software, client libraries, and so on. XSF can be found at http://xmpp.org/. Specifically, all XMPP extensions can be found at http://xmpp.org/extensions/.

Procedural extensions that are accepted for publication pass through three levels of acceptance. First, there is the experimental stage where an extension is recognized as the factor that would provide a solution for an important use case but is still under discussion and can undergo significant changes in the process. The next step is the draft stage where the extension has undergone extensive discussion and technical review. Any changes made to an extension in this stage should always be made in a backward-compatible manner if possible. The last stage is the final stage where changes are no longer made.

At the time of writing this, there is a sequence of new experimental extensions published by XSF, aimed at IoT. We will use these extensions in our examples. To improve interoperability, the source code for the implementation of these extensions has also been included in the `Clayster.Library.IoT` library. These extensions include extensions to communicate with sensor data or control actuators, sending asynchronous events based on subscriber-specific conditions. They also include extensions to register devices securely and provision the services in the networks. Furthermore, all our examples will avoid the storage of sensitive information centrally. Instead, data will be made available on request and only given to a trusted few by the owner-approved parties.

## Connecting to a server

There are various methods available to connect to an XMPP server. The most common method, the one we will use in the examples in this book, is for a client to connect through a normal TCP socket connection to either `xmpp-client` service if access to DNS-SRV records is available, or port 5222 if not. XML fragments are then transported in both the directions, as described in RFC 6120-6122.

> EXI compression can be negotiated over this connection if supported by the server. An alternative binding method is to connect to the `xmpp-bclient` service directly to avoid having to switch over from XML to an EXI compressed XML.

An alternative way to connect to an XMPP server is by using **Bidirectional streams Over Synchronous HTTP (BOSH)**. This allows clients with access to only the HTTP protocol to use XMPP as well. Some servers also publish XMPP over web socket interfaces. This makes it possible to access the XMPP network for clients, such as web browsers and so on.

XMPP servers also receive connections from other XMPP servers. This is part of the federation feature of XMPP. These servers connect to each other using the `xmpp-server` service name if DNS-SRV records are available, or port 5269 if not.

A final method worth mentioning to connect to a server is through a special port (5275) that the server components can connect to. This port must not be open on the Internet but can be used to extend the functionality of the XMPP server, as described earlier. The following diagram displays the functionality of the XMPP server with respect to the Internet architecture:

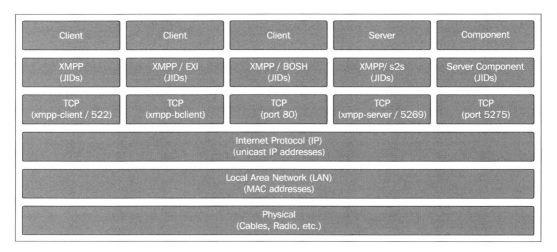

## Provisioning for added security

In this chapter, we will introduce several new communication patterns that are useful for things in IoT. One such paradigm is the creation of identity, where things by themselves create their own identity on the network. Once a thing has created an identity on the network, we will introduce a way to register the thing, discover it, and safely claim ownership of it. Once the ownership has been claimed, we can then use the provisioning extension to delegate trust to a trusted third party, a provisioning server, which we will then use to control who can connect to our devices and what they can do.

To achieve discovery and provisioning, which work as server components, we will need support from a server that hosts such components. For this reason, we will use the XMPP server available at `thingk.me`. This server also has a web interface at `http://thingk.me/` where users can control their claimed devices.

# Adding XMPP support to a thing

We are now ready to start implementing support for XMPP in our devices. We will begin with the sensor. Most of the implementation needed is generic and will be reused in all our projects created so far. Device-specific interfaces will be described afterwards. The `Clayster.Library.Internet.XMPP` namespace has an XMPP client that allows us to communicate using the XMPP primitives and register custom message handlers and IQ handlers.

# Connecting to the XMPP network

To connect to the XMPP network, we first need to instantiate an XMPP client. To do this, we need a `JID`, a password, the name of the XMPP server and its port number, and the ISO code of the default language we use by default:

```
xmppClient = new XmppClient (xmppSettings.Jid,
   xmppSettings.Password, xmppSettings.Host,
   xmppSettings.Port, "en");
```

If automatic account creation is supported by the server but requires a signature to make sure malicious account creation is not allowed, you also need to provide a key and secret. Such a key and secret is obtained by the corresponding service provider. If not supported or desired, you can omit these lines of code:

```
xmppClient.SignatureKey = xmppSettings.ManufacturerKey;
xmppClient.SignatureSecret = xmppSettings.ManufacturerSecret;
```

> Automatic account creation is defined in the XMPP extension XEP-0077: In-band Registration. Signing account creation requests is defined in the XMPP extension XEP-0348: Signing Forms.

When connecting to an XMPP server, the client will validate the certificate provided by the server to make sure it corresponds to the domain. If, for some reason, the certificate does not validate, the default action is to abort the connection attempt. If you connect to a server where you know the certificate does not validate the domain or if the certificate is self-signed, you can override this validation as follows:

```
xmppClient.TrustCertificates = true;
```

> To make certificates validate properly on Raspberry Pi, you might need to install CA certificates on the device. Refer to *Appendix O, Certificates and Validation*, for more information on how to do this.

Additionally, if you want to view the actual communication that takes place, you need to register a line listener with the client in the same way you did for other protocols:

```
xmppClient.RegisterLineListener (
  new ConsoleOutLineListenerSink (BinaryFormat.ByteCount));
```

Finally, we open the connection as follows. The parameter to the `Open` method tells the client that we will allow an account to be created if it is not found on the server. If an account is created, it will be done so using the credentials already provided:

```
xmppClient.Open (true);
```

When terminating the application, it is important to call the static `Terminate` method on the `XmppClient` class. This method makes sure the heart beat thread is gracefully terminated. This thread ensures the connections are alive even when nothing is being communicated:

```
XmppClient.Terminate ();
```

## Monitoring connection state events

All the operations in XMPP are asynchronous. This means that the `Open` method we just discussed only starts the connection process. Any state changes, successes, or failures are reported by raising different events. There are various event handlers defined on the XMPP client that the application can use to keep track of the state and progress of the connection attempt.

To learn whether an account was successfully created, we can register an event handler on the `OnAccountRegistrationSuccessful` event. In the same way, we can use the `OnAccountRegistrationFailed` event to detect a permanent failure when an account is not found and a new account could not be created:

```
xmppClient.OnAccountRegistrationFailed += (Client, Form) =>
{
  xmppPermanentFailure = true;
  Client.Close ();
};
```

> During the life cycle of a client, we can monitor how the client changes between the `Offline`, `Connecting`, `Authenticating`, `Connected`, and `Error` states by using an `OnStateChange` event handler.

## Notifying your friends

Once the client has been successfully authenticated by the server (or an account created), the `OnConnected` event is raised. The first thing we must do once this is done is set the desired presence of the client. This presence will be distributed to friends subscribing to presence notifications to alert them of the new status of the connection. It will also alert them of the current resource bound to the connection, enabling them to communicate with your application. This is done as follows:

```
xmppClient.OnConnected += (Client) =>
{
  Client.SetPresence (PresenceStatus.Online);
```

## Handling HTTP requests over XMPP

We have defined a lot of HTTP resources in the previous chapters. It is possible for the web server to serve HTTP requests that come over XMPP connections as well. By calling the following method during application initialization, HTTP requests can be served, both by clients with IP access to the device (normal HTTP) and friends over the XMPP network.

```
HttpServer.RegisterHttpOverXmppSupport (6000, 1024 * 1024);
```

The first number represents the maximum number of bytes to be sent in a single message and should result in messages smaller than the smallest maximum allowed stanza size (10000 bytes). If a response is larger, a chunked service will be used, where the response will be divided into chunks and sent in a sequence of messages. As chunks are base64-encoded, 6000 bytes are encoded as 8000 bytes, leaving some margin for the XML encapsulating the chunk. The second number is an upper limit for the chunked service where the corresponding content should be transferred using a streaming option instead. In our examples, HTTP requests over XMPP will be used to fetch the camera picture from our camera device. It already has an HTTP resource to retrieve a camera image. Using this single method call, we will make sure it is possible to retrieve the same image over the XMPP network as well.

HTTP over XMPP transport is defined in an extension called XEP-0332: HTTP over XMPP transport.

# Providing an additional layer of security

We are now theoretically ready to communicate with anybody who is our friend. But who can we be friends with? Who is allowed to befriend us? What are they allowed to read or control once they are befriended? Should we pre-program this? Should friendships be manually configured using another XMPP client, such as a chat client, or should we build in logic for this to be configured remotely? These questions are important to consider during the architectural design phase of a project. We don't just want anybody to be able to connect to the device and do anything with it.

Things connected to the Internet differ a lot in various ways from other machines that are connected to the Internet but operated by humans. Some of them are listed as follows:

- Things need to make all the decisions without help from a human operator.
- It might be difficult to update the firmware on the device, compared to updating software on a PC.
- Multiple things probably collaborate together at the same time, forming part of a larger eco-system. It might be easy to control settings in one device, but how do you administer multiple devices across the Internet? Do you want to log in to each one and set them individually?

# The basics of provisioning

Instead of making an implementation that will handle all the considerations we just discussed into each device we will create, we will take the opportunity to use another method in this chapter. In this method, we will delegate trust to a third party called provisioning server and let it tell each device what is permitted and to what extent. Instead of trying to implement individual privacy solutions in each device we will create, we will delegate this responsibility to a trusted third party where it is both easier and more practical to implement security decision logic than doing this in each device. It is also easier for the owner of the things to administrate since all the rules can be configured in one place. And it does not violate privacy or integrity of data since the provisioning server only stores simple rules concerning who can talk to whom and about what, not the actual data that belongs to the owner, which can be sensitive.

The principle is easy: if somebody wants to do something with the device, the device asks the provisioning server whether it is allowed and to what extent. When the response is returned from the provisioning server, the device responds to the original request accordingly. If the question is new, the provisioning server flags the owner that a new situation has arisen that it needs input on. The owner then responds, and the provisioning server learns and uses this knowledge to respond to future questions of the same sort.

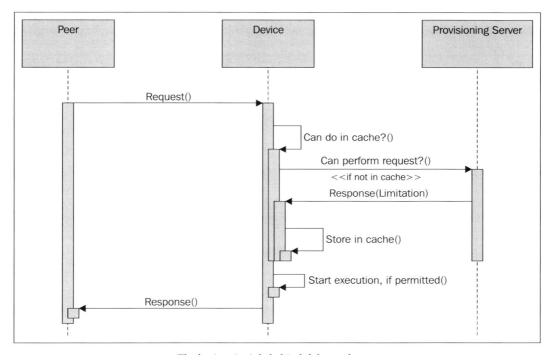

The basic principle behind delegated trust

 To avoid bottlenecks, the device actually only asks once for each new type of request it receives and then remembers the response. The provisioning server can then ask the device to forget the previous responses if the rules were to change. The details of how the provisioning protocol works is described in the XMPP extension called XEP-0324: IoT - Provisioning.

Before the provisioning server can give any meaningful responses to queries, the provisioning server needs to know who the device actually is and who its owner is. This connection between the thing's identity and owner is done by a Thing Registry. The thing first registers itself, possibly with its newly created identity together with some information or metadata about itself.

Then, it provides this metadata to its owner in some way. We will do this using a QR code that contains the metadata that is encoded. It is assumed that anybody who has access to this code (which might be on a sticker on the box) and presents it first to the registry is also the owner of the thing. So, the owner scans the QR code and sends an ownership claim to the registry, which then returns a receipt with the JID of the thing, if claimed. The registry also informs the thing that the thing has been claimed and who its owner is.

QR code is discussed in more detail in *Appendix Q, QR-Code*. Thing registries and how things register themselves and are discovered is further described in the XMPP extension called XEP-0347: IoT - Discovery.

Once the thing has been claimed by an owner, the provisioning server knows who can decide what the thing is allowed to do.

## Initializing the Thing Registry interface

At this point, we will assume we know the address of the Thing Registry interface we want to use. We keep the address in `xmppSettings.ThingRegistry`. So, before we open the XMPP connection, we check whether we have an address and call a special setup method to initialize the Thing Registry interface:

```
if (!string.IsNullOrEmpty (xmppSettings.ThingRegistry))
   SetupThingRegistry ();
```

A class named `ThingRegistry` helps us handle communication with a Thing Registry and is defined in the `Clayster.Library.IoT.Provisioning` namespace. It has three events we need to provide handlers for. `OnClaimed` event is raised when the device has been claimed by its owner. `OnRemoved` event is raised when the owner removes the device from the registry database but maintains ownership of the device. Finally, the `OnDisowned` event is raised when the owner disowns the thing, making it possible for the thing to be claimed by a new owner. This can be done as follows:

```
private static void SetupThingRegistry ()
{
   xmppRegistry = new ThingRegistry (xmppClient,
     xmppSettings.ThingRegistry);
   xmppRegistry.OnClaimed += OnClaimed;
   xmppRegistry.OnRemoved += OnRemoved;
   xmppRegistry.OnDisowned += OnDisowned;
}
```

# Registering a thing

To facilitate registration of the device from different parts of the code, we need to create a method for it. A Thing Registry has two purposes. The first is to match things with their owners. The second is to be a bulletin board of public things. A public thing is a thing that has been successfully claimed that the owner agrees to make public. Public things can be searched for using the tags provided by them, including numerical tags such as location. So we need to differ between registering a thing without an owner and registering an update for a public thing that has an owner. As shown in the following code, we begin with a case where the thing doesn't have an owner yet:

```
private static void RegisterDevice ()
{
   if (xmppRegistry != null)
   {
     if (string.IsNullOrEmpty (xmppSettings.Owner))
     {
```

We continue by performing a registration, which is simple. The device simply registers a set of tags, comprising metadata about the device. The tags will become associated with the JID of the sender at the registry. Each tag has a name and a value. The value can be either a string or a number. The first parameter to the `Register` method tells the registry whether the device is self-owned or not. This is shown in the following code:

```
xmppRegistry.Register (false,
   new StringTag ("MAN", "clayster.com"),
   new StringTag ("MODEL", "LearningIoT-Sensor"),
   new StringTag ("KEY", xmppSettings.Key));
```

> A special tag named `KEY` is neither displayed to anybody, nor is it searchable. It is also removed from the registry once the thing has been claimed. The purpose is to provide a random string, such as a GUID, unique to the thing itself. The thing can be claimed only with access to the complete set of tags.
>
> Any tag names can be used. But there exists a list of predefined tag names for interoperability between things. These are listed in XEP-0347; refer to http://xmpp.org/extensions/xep-0347.html#tags.
>
> A registration will only be effective if the thing is not claimed before. If claimed, the request is ignored by the registry and the `OnClaimed` event will be raised with the JID of the current owner.
>
> Also, note that a successful registration removes all the previous metadata in the registry corresponding to the JID of the sender.

## Updating a public thing

If the thing has an owner and it is public, we make a similar call where we register updates to the metadata. In this case, previous metadata will be updated, and the tags that are not available in the request will be maintained as they are. We also avoid using the KEY tag as seen in the following code:

```
   }
   else if (xmppSettings.Public)
   {
     xmppRegistry.Update (
       new StringTag ("MAN", "clayster.com"),
       new StringTag ("MODEL", "LearningIoT-Sensor"),
       new NumericalTag ("LAT", -32.976425),
       new NumericalTag ("LON", -71.531690));
   }
}
```

## Claiming a thing

Once the thing is claimed, the OnClaimed event is raised. This event contains information about who the owner is and whether the owner has chosen to keep the thing private or publish it as a public thing in the registry. We update our internal settings with this information and call the RegisterDevice method to update the metadata in the registry accordingly. This is shown in the next code snippet:

```
private static void OnClaimed (object Sender, ClaimedEventArgs e)
{
  xmppSettings.Owner = e.Owner;
  xmppSettings.Public = e.Public;
  xmppSettings.UpdateIfModified ();

  RegisterDevice ();
}
```

## Removing a thing from the registry

The owner (or the thing) can remove the thing from the Thing Registry and thus make it private. When this happens, the OnRemoved event is raised. Since the thing is now private, it doesn't need to update the registry with any metadata any longer. We update our information as follows:

```
private static void OnRemoved
   (object Sender,NodeReferenceEventArgs e)
```

```
{
  xmppSettings.Public = false;
  xmppSettings.UpdateIfModified ();
}
```

## Disowning a thing

If an owner wants to pass on the ownership of the device to another or give it away, the owner starts by disowning the thing in the provisioning server. When this happens, the `OnDisowned` event is raised:

```
private static void OnDisowned (object Sender,
   NodeReferenceEventArgs e)
{
  xmppSettings.Owner = string.Empty;
  xmppSettings.Public = false;
  xmppSettings.UpdateIfModified ();
```

In our event, we also remove the owner from our roster. This makes sure that the previous owner will not be able access the device again without the permission of the new owner. This is done as follows:

```
string Jid = XMPPSettings.Owner;
if (!string.IsNullOrEmpty (Jid))
{
  XmppContact Contact = xmppClient.GetLocalContact (Jid);
  if (Contact != null)
    xmppClient.DeleteContact (Contact);
}
```

In this event, it is also important to re-register the thing so that it gets an opportunity to be reclaimed. We also make sure we display the QR code again since it gives the new owner a chance to see and use it to claim the device. The QR code is displayed again with the following code:

```
  RegisterDevice ();
  if (xmppSettings.QRCode != null)
    DisplayQRCode ();
}
```

 QR code is discussed in more detail in *Appendix Q, QR-Code*.

## Initializing the provisioning server interface

In the same way as for the Thing Registry interface, we set up the provisioning server interface if we have an address for it. This is done before we open the XMPP connection with the following code:

```
if (!string.IsNullOrEmpty (xmppSettings.ProvisioningServer))
   SetupProvisioningServer ();
```

The `ProvisioningServer` class in the `Clayster.Library.IoT.Provisioning` namespace handles communication with the provisioning server. Apart from a reference to our XMPP client and the address to the provisioning server, this class takes a third parameter, representing the number of unique questions to remember the answers for in the provisioning cache. Questions represent friendship requests, readout requests, and control requests, and the number should represent a number that can be stored and still encompass the estimated number of different queries expected in a normal operation to avoid spamming the provisioning server. Using a cache this way makes sure that each unique question is only forwarded to the provisioning server once, as long as rules do not change. This can be done with the following code snippet:

```
private static void SetupProvisioningServer ()
{
   xmppProvisioningServer = new ProvisioningServer
      (xmppClient, xmppSettings.ProvisioningServer, 1000);
```

The provisioning server interface also has two events we should provide event handlers for. The `OnFriend` event is raised when the provisioning server recommends a new friendship, and `OnUnfriend` is raised when an existing friendship needs to be removed. This is done as follows:

```
xmppProvisioningServer.OnFriend += OnFriend;
xmppProvisioningServer.OnUnfriend += OnUnfriend;
```

## Handling friendship recommendations

In the `OnFriend` event, we receive a `JID` of a recommended friendship. To create a friendship, we start by subscribing to its presence. The contact will make a decision whether to accept or deny the presence subscription request. If it accepts the presence subscription request, it will probably send a presence subscription request back to the sender as well. When both have accepted each other's presence subscriptions, we will see them as friends:

```
private static void OnFriend (object Sender, JidEventArgs e)
{
```

```
      xmppClient.RequestPresenceSubscription (e.Jid);
   }
```

## Handling requests to unfriend somebody

The `OnUnfriend` event is raised when the provisioning server recommends that you remove an existing friendship. You can do this easily by simply removing the corresponding contact from your roster:

```
   private static void OnUnfriend (object Sender, JidEventArgs e)
   {
      XmppContact Contact = xmppClient.GetLocalContact (e.Jid);
      if (Contact != null)
         xmppClient.DeleteContact (Contact);
   }
```

## Searching for a provisioning server

Previously, we assumed that we know the address of the Thing Registry or the provisioning server. But what if we don't? We can have it pre-programmed or preconfigured or deduce it from the domain of the XMPP server. It can be a JID or a server component address. If a Thing Registry or provisioning server is hosted as components on the current XMPP server, we can also find it dynamically by going through all the published components and analyzing their capabilities. In our applications, we will use the latter because the XMPP server at `thingk.me` hosts both the Thing Registry and provisioning server as a subcomponent on the same server.

To start a search for the components on the server, we will issue a standard service discovery request to the server. We will do this in the `OnConnected` event handler, right after having our presence status set if a Thing Registry or provisioning server has not been initialized already:

```
   if (xmppRegistry == null || xmppProvisioningServer == null)
      Client.RequestServiceDiscovery (string.Empty,
         XmppServiceDiscoveryResponse, null);
```

The response to this query will contain a set of features. The available components are reported as items. So, we need to check whether such items are supported by the server, and if they are, perform a service items discovery request to the server, as follows.

```
   private static void XmppServiceDiscoveryResponse (
      XmppClient Client, XmppServiceDiscoveryEventArgs e)
   {
```

## The XMPP Protocol

```
    if (Array.IndexOf<string> (e.Features,
      XmppClient.NamespaceDiscoveryItems) >= 0)
    Client.RequestServiceDiscoveryItems (Client.Domain,
      XmppServiceDiscoveryItemsResponse, null);
}
```

The response will contain a set of items. We loop through this and perform an individual service discovery request on each item, if it has a JID, to learn what features are supported by each one. This is done with the following code:

```
private static void XmppServiceDiscoveryItemsResponse
  (XmppClient Client, XmppServiceDiscoveryItemsEventArgs e)
{
  foreach (XmppServiceDiscoveryItem Item in e.Items)
  {
    if (!string.IsNullOrEmpty (Item.Jid))
      Client.RequestServiceDiscovery (Item.Jid, Item.Node,
        XmppServiceDiscoveryItemResponse, Item);
  }
}
```

In each response, we check the Features array to confirm whether the urn:Xmpp:iot:discovery namespace is present. If it is, it means the corresponding Jid is an address to a Thing Registry:

```
private static void XmppServiceDiscoveryItemResponse
  (XmppClient Client, XmppServiceDiscoveryEventArgs e)
{
  XmppServiceDiscoveryItem Item =
    (XMPPServiceDiscoveryItem)e.State;
  if (Array.IndexOf<string>
    (e.Features, "urn:xmpp:iot:discovery") >= 0)
  {
    XmppSettings.ThingRegistry = Item.Jid;
    SetupThingRegistry ();
  }
```

In the same way, we can check for the presence of the urn:xmpp:iot:provisioning namespace. If it is, it means the corresponding JID is an address to a provisioning server:

```
  if (Array.IndexOf<string> (e.Features,
    "urn:xmpp:iot:provisioning") >= 0)
  {
    xmppSettings.ProvisioningServer = Item.Jid;
    SetupProvisioningServer ();
  }
```

# Providing registry information

We can now update our information accordingly. If we have found a Thing Registry, we make sure to display a QR code for the owner. If not available, we request for one. Finally, we register the device in the registry as follows:

```
xmppSettings.UpdateIfModified ();
if (!string.IsNullOrEmpty (xmppSettings.ThingRegistry))
{
  if (xmppSettings.QRCode == null)
    RequestQRCode ();
  else if (string.IsNullOrEmpty (xmppSettings.Owner))
    DisplayQRCode ();

  RegisterDevice ();
}
```

We need to provide similar logic at the end of our `OnConnected` event handler if a Thing Registry and provisioning server address are already configured and a service discovery request is not issued.

Now both the owner and the registry have sufficient information to claim the device.

> QR code is discussed in more detail in *Appendix Q, QR-Code*.

# Maintaining a connection

For a device to be able to receive requests, it needs to ensure its connection is open. In a network, a lot can happen. Servers and network could go down, services might need to be updated, and power could fail. All these things lead to the connection being dropped. For this reason, it is important to manage these events and try to reconnect. The first thing we can do is try to reconnect when a working connection is dropped. We can do this in a response to an `OnClosed` event if no permanent error is detected.

If this does not work and a connection is not possible for some time, we need to regularly check the state of the connection using some arbitrary interval. In our downloadable example code, every minute we check for either a missing connection or whether the client is in an `Error` or `Offline` state. If so, we recycle the connection by closing it and opening it again.

# Negotiating friendships

A friendship between two peers in XMPP is where both peers subscribe to each other's presence. In order to negotiate such friendships, special presence stanzas are sent between each peer. The friendship negotiation involves the XMPP servers of each device, and negotiation is done using bare JIDs. The following illustration shows a simplified sequence of a friendship negotiation between two peers, where we only involve the two peers and hide the implicit server communication that also takes place.

The four specific presence types used are Subscribe, Subscribed, Unsubscribe, and Unsubscribed. To subscribe to the presence of somebody else, or "ask to be friends with them," you send a Subscribe presence stanza to its bare JID. If you want to accept such a request, you respond with a Subscribed presence stanza; if not, you respond with an Unsubscribed presence stanza. To unsubscribe your presence subscription, you send an Unsubscribe presence stanza. But this is not the same as removing the friendship since the other may continue to subscribe to your presence. If you want to remove a friendship, it's better to delete the contact from the roster directly. The following diagram shows the simplified friendship negotiations:

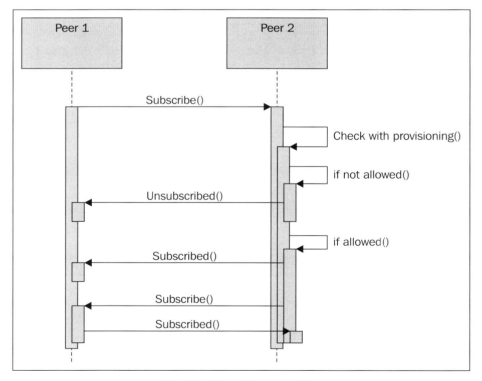

Simplified friendship negotiation

# Handling presence subscription requests

We implement the logic explained in the previous section in an event handler for the `OnPresenceReceived` event as follows:

```
xmppClient.OnPresenceReceived += (Client, Presence) =>
{
  switch (Presence.Type)
  {
```

We begin with presence subscription requests. If we are not connected with a provisioning server that helps us decide with whom we can connect, we will reject all the incoming requests with the following code:

```
case PresenceType.Subscribe:
  if (xmppProvisioningServer == null)
    Client.RefusePresenceSubscription (Presence.From);
```

If a provisioning server is detected, we ask it whether we can be friends with the peer requesting the subscription:

```
else
{
  xmppProvisioningServer.IsFriend (Presence.From, e =>
  {
```

If the provisioning server approves the friendship, we accept the presence subscription and return a request of a presence subscription of our new protofriend if it is a peer, that is, it has a JID and not only a domain or subdomain address. The request can be sent as follows:

```
if (e.Result)
{
  Client.AcceptPresenceSubscription (Presence.From);
  if (Presence.From.IndexOf ('@') > 0)
    Client.RequestPresenceSubscription (Presence.From);
```

If the provisioning server does not approve of the friendship, we simply refuse the subscription and delete the contact:

```
}
else
{
  Client.RefusePresenceSubscription (Presence.From);
  XmppContact Contact = xmppClient.GetLocalContact
    (Presence.From);
```

```
      if (Contact != null)
        xmppClient.DeleteContact (Contact);
    }
  }, null);
}
break;
```

If a peer requests to unsubscribe from its presence subscription to our device, we simply acknowledge the request:

```
case PresenceType.Unsubscribe:
  Client.AcceptPresenceUnsubscription (Presence.From);
break;
```

The received presence stanzas of the type `Subscribed` and `Unsubscribed` are receipts we receive after a peer has processed our requests. In our application, we don't need to react to these.

# Continuing interrupted negotiations

Since friendship relationships are negotiated using multiple asynchronous messages, things can go wrong if one or both of the peers are interrupted or their connections closed during the process. It is important to have this possibility in mind. Fortunately, it is easy to recover from such interruptions. When the client connects, it loads its roster from the server. The roster contains all the JIDs' contacts and their corresponding presence subscription status. The `OnRosterReceived` event is raised when the XMPP client has received the roster from the server after having connected successfully.

To continue with interrupted negotiations, we can add an event handler for this event and loop through all the contacts received to see whether any one of them has unfinished friendship negotiations. Each contact will have an `Ask` property, and if this is set to `Subscribe`, it would mean that the contact is asking to subscribe to our presence. We can handle it as a new incoming friendship request.

It can also be so that the contact is successfully subscribed to our presence but we are not subscribed to the presence of the contact. The `Subscription` property of each contact tells us who subscribes to whom. In a friendship relationship, the value is `Both`. But if the value is `To` or `From`, only one is subscribed to the other. `From` means a presence subscription from the contact of your presence exists. Is it because we should be friends or because we're unfriending the contact? We need to ask the provisioning server, and if allowed, we continue and request for the presence subscription from the contact. Otherwise, we properly delete the contact from the roster.

# Adding XMPP support to the sensor

Now that we have the devices connected to the XMPP network, adding the appropriate sensor interfaces is easy. The `Clayster.Library.IoT.XmppInterfaces` namespace contains a series of classes that handle most of the interfaces we need.

## Adding a sensor server interface

The XMPP extension XEP-0323: IoT – Sensor Data specifies how sensor data can be interchanged over the XMPP network. It defines a request/response model, similar to the one we have used already, where a client asks a server for sensor data. In our sensor, we therefore create an `XmppSensorServer` object as soon as we have both an XMPP client created and a provisioning server defined. Its `OnReadout` event is raised whenever data is to be sent somewhere. All of the negotiation with the provisioning server has already been taken care of, including the possible limitations of the original request. This is done with the help of the following code:

```
xmppSensorServer = new XmppSensorServer (xmppClient,
   xmppProvisioningServer);
xmppSensorServer.OnReadout += OnReadout;
```

The actual readout of the sensor is simple. It fits into our already defined sensor data export we use for other protocols. We simply call the `ExportSensorData` method defined in previous chapters.

> For an example on how you can access these sensor values through a chat session with the sensor, refer to *Appendix P, Chat Interfaces*.

## Updating event subscriptions

The `XmppSensorServer` class also handles event subscriptions according to a ProtoXEP: IoT – Events. This makes it possible for clients to request for sensor data based on the change in conditions. To make sure all subscriptions are updated accordingly, we need to inform the sensor server interface when new momentary values are available. We do this as follows:

```
if (XMPPSensorServer != null)
{
```

```
xmppSensorServer.MomentaryValuesUpdated (
    new KeyValuePair<string, double> (
      "Temperature", temperatureC),
    new KeyValuePair<string, double> (
      "Light", lightPercent),
    new KeyValuePair<string, double> (
      "Motion", motionDetected ? 1 : 0));
}
```

> This extension has not been approved by the XSF at the time of writing this. Anyway, it can be used as a simple way to subscribe to sensor data events, but with conditions. You can view this work in progress at http://xmpp.org/extensions/inbox/iot-events.html.

## Publishing contracts

When things interconnect, they need to analyze each other to see what capabilities they have. One way to do this is to use the XMPP service discovery query to figure out what it features. When the sensor is queried by a peer, it will learn that it is a sensor and that it can be read. But what values are supported? One way to find this out is to read the sensor and see what it supports. However, this requires some extensive analysis of incoming data, which may vary in content and order. Another method is to retrieve a list of interoperability interfaces or contracts, as defined by a ProtoXEP: IoT - Interoperability. Here, each reference corresponds to a contract, as shown in the next code, where the sender promises to work in accordance with the corresponding contract:

```
xmppInteroperabilityServer = new XmppInteroperabilityServer (
    xmppClient,
    "XMPP.IoT.Sensor.Temperature",
    "XMPP.IoT.Sensor.Temperature.History",
    "Clayster.LearningIoT.Sensor.Light",
    "Clayster.LearningIoT.Sensor.Light.History",
    "Clayster.LearningIoT.Sensor.Motion",
    "Clayster.LearningIoT.Sensor.Motion.History");
```

All contracts are ordered into the form of a tree structure. Contracts that begin with XMPP.IoT are defined in the proto-XEP. But you can define any contract you want. In our example, we inform the interested party that the sensor is a temperature sensor that supports historical values. We also define our own light sensor and motion sensor contracts with History. These will be used later by the controller to easily detect whether the connected peer is the sensor it is looking for.

This extension has not been sent to the XSF and therefore neither approved nor published by the XSF. It can be used anyway as a simple way to interchange references with contracts between things. You can view this work in progress at http://htmlpreview.github.io/?https://github.com/joachimlindborg/XMPP-IoT/blob/master/xep-0000-IoT-Interoperability.html.

# Adding XMPP support to the actuator

Like with the sensor project, adding the final interfaces for our actuator is a minor task. The device will register itself as LearningIoT-Actuator instead of LearningIoT-Sensor for instance. Adding a sensor server interface to the actuator is done in more or less the same way as described for the sensor, except that the names and types of the fields and momentary values are different. In this section, we will discuss the actuator-specific interfaces that need to be considered.

The contracts we will use for the actuator are as follows:

```
xmppInteroperabilityServer = new XmppInteroperabilityServer (
  xmppClient,
  "XMPP.IoT.Actuator.DigitalOutputs",
  "XMPP.IoT.Security.Alarm",
  "Clayster.LearningIoT.Actuator.DO1-8");
```

## Adding a controller server interface

The XMPP extension XEP-0325: IoT - Control specifies how control operations in IoT can be performed using the XMPP protocol. It defines an asynchronous messaging model and a parallel request/response model, where a client sends control commands to a server. The client can also request for a set of available controllable parameters in the server. There is a class we can use that implements this extension for us. It is called XmppControlServer.

In our actuator, we therefore create an instance of this class as soon as we have both an XMPP client created and a provisioning server defined. The constructor requires a list of control parameters defining what parameters should be controllable through the interface. These parameters should match the corresponding fields that are readable through the sensor server interface. Each control parameter is defined by the following parameters:

- Data type of the underlying value
- Control parameter's name
- The current value

- Delegate to the callback method, which is called when the parameter is read
- Delegate to the callback method, which is called when the parameter is set
- A title string
- A tooltip string
- Possible range

Some of the parameters are used when creating a control form for the corresponding parameters, and they are meant for end users and for input form validation. The `Clayster.Library.IoT.XmppInterfaces.ControlParameters` namespace contains classes for the different types of control parameters supported by XEP-0325. We create our control server as follows. We've replaced a sequence of repetitive parameters with an ellipsis ("..."):

```
xmppControlServer = new XmppControlServer (
   xmppClient, xmppProvisioningServer,
   new BooleanControlParameter ("Digital Output 1",
      () => wsApi.GetDigitalOutput (1),
      (v) => wsApi.SetDigitalOutput (1, v),
      "Digital Output 1:", "State of digital output 1."),
   ...,
   new BooleanControlParameter ("Digital Output 8",
      () => wsApi.GetDigitalOutput (8),
      (v) => wsApi.SetDigitalOutput (8, v),
      "Digital Output 8:", "State of digital output 8."),
   new BooleanControlParameter ("State",
      () => wsApi.GetAlarmOutput (),
      (v) => wsApi.SetAlarmOutput (v),
      "Alarm Output:","State of the alarm output."),
   new Int32ControlParameter ("Digital Outputs",
      () => (int)wsApi.GetDigitalOutputs (),
      (v) => wsApi.SetDigitalOutputs ((byte)v),
      "Digital Outputs:", "State of all digital outputs.",
      0, 255));
```

# Adding XMPP support to the camera

Enabling XMPP in our camera is also easy, except that we will register our camera as `LearningIoT-Camera` instead of `LearningIoT-Sensor`. Previously, our camera has only worked in the local area network using UPnP. Since UPnP is based on HTTP, the camera image will be automatically available over XMPP if we make sure to activate HTTP over XMPP support, as described earlier in this chapter.

We also need to provide a sensor interface with an event infrastructure, similar to the one provided by UPnP. The simplest way to do this is by converting the camera into a sensor and reporting the corresponding camera parameters as sensor data fields. Since the sensor data model supports events, we can achieve the same thing over XMPP like we did with local HTTP using UPnP. The actual implementation closely mimics what we did with the sensor project, and we refer interested readers to the downloadable source code for the project if they are interested in the details.

# Adding XMPP support to the controller

The controller project is different from the previous projects in that it will be a client of the other three projects. It will still need to register itself (using the model name `LearningIoT-Controller`) with the Thing Registry and use provisioning where applicable so that the provisioning server can be used to connect all the devices together by recommending who should befriend whom.

## Setting up a sensor client interface

Once we have the `JID` of the sensor, we can request for or subscribe to data from it using the `XmppSensorClient` class:

```
xmppSensorClient = new XmppSensorClient (xmppClient);
```

## Subscribing to sensor data

We initialize our relationship with the sensor by subscribing to the `Light` and `Motion` field values from it using the following code. We also specify that we want information when the light has changed to one unit of a percent, or if the motion has changed from true to false (which corresponds to a numerical change of one).

```
private static void InitSensor (string Jid)
{
  xmppSensorClient.SubscribeData (-1, Jid,
    ReadoutType.MomentaryValues, null, new FieldCondition[]
  {
    FieldCondition.IfChanged ("Light", 1),
      FieldCondition.IfChanged ("Motion", 1)
  },
  null, null, new Duration (0, 0, 0, 0, 1, 0), true,
    string.Empty, string.Empty, string.Empty,NewSensorData, null);
}
```

# The XMPP Protocol

The subscription call takes a sequence of parameters, as follows:

- An optional sequence number (-1) that can be used to identify the subscription.
- The Jid of the sensor.
- The types of fields you want.
- Any underlying nodes to read (null in our case since the sensor is not a concentrator).
- A set of fields with optional conditions to subscribe to.
- An optional maximum age (null) of the historical data that is subscribed to. Since we don't subscribe to historical data, we can leave this as null.
- An optional minimum interval time (null), setting a limit on how fast messages can be sent to us.
- An optional maximum interval time (1 minute), making sure we receive messages at least this frequently.
- If an immediate request is desired (true), sensor data will be sent immediately as soon as the subscription has been accepted.
- A triple of security tokens representing the service, device, and unit. This can be used for extended identification with the provisioning server or if the subscription is a result of an external request and the identity of the requester is forwarded. We leave these as empty strings since the subscription is made directly from the controller.
- A callback method to call when the sensor data has been received as a result of the subscription.
- A state object to pass on to the callback method.

> If you only want data once, you can use the RequestData method instead of the SubscribeData method. It takes similar parameters.

## Handling incoming sensor data

Sensor data will have been parsed correctly before being passed on to the callback method provided. It will be available in the event arguments, as shown in the next code:

```
private static void NewSensorData
   (object Sender,SensorDataEventArgs e)
{
   FieldNumeric Num;
   FieldBoolean Bool;
```

In theory, sensor data can be reported in a sequence of messages, depending on how the sensor reads and processes field values and also the amount of values reported. The callback method will be called once for every message. The Done property lets you know whether the message is the last message in a sequence. Field values in the most recent message will be available in the RecentFields property, while the sum of all the fields during the readout is available in the TotalFields property. In our case, it is sufficient to loop through the the fields reported in the most recent message:

```
if (e.HasRecentFields)
{
  foreach (Field Field in e.RecentFields)
  {
```

Checking incoming fields is straightforward:

```
if (Field.FieldName == "Light" &&
  (Num = Field as FieldNumeric) != null &&
  Num.Unit == "%" && Num.Value >= 0 && Num.Value <= 100)
    lightPercent = Num.Value;
else if (Field.FieldName == "Motion" &&
  (Bool = Field as FieldBoolean) != null)
    motion = Bool.Value;
```

We end by checking the control rules as follows to see whether the state of the system has changed:

```
  }
  hasValues = true;
  CheckControlRules ();
 }
}
```

## Setting up a controller client interface

Communicating with the actuator is simply done using the XmppControlClient class with the help of a controller interface:

```
xmppControlClient = new XmppControlClient (xmppClient);
```

Controlling parameters can be done in two ways: either through a control form or individual parameter set operations. The control form will contain all the controllable parameters and can also be used to see whether a parameter exists, what type it has, and what its boundary values are. It can also be used to set a group of parameters at once.

During the initialization of our actuator interface, we request the control form as follows:

```
private static void InitActuator (string Jid)
{
   xmppControlClient.GetForm (Jid, ControlFormResponse, Jid);
}
```

We handle the response in the following manner. If the Form property is null in the event arguments, an error will be reported:

```
private static void ControlFormResponse (object Sender,
   ControlFormEventArgs e)
{
   string Jid = (string)e.State;
   if (e.Form != null)
   {
      ...
   }
   else
      Log.Error (e.ErrorMessage, EventLevel.Major, Jid);
}
```

We will use the form mainly to know what parameters are available in the actuator and use individual set operations to control them. Both individual set operations and a group parameter set operation, which use a control form, are done using the overloaded versions of the Set method in the XmppControlClient class. The version that is used depends of the data type of the value parameter passed to the method. Setting up our digital output in the form of our integer control parameter is done as follows:

```
if (i >= 0 && xmppControlForm.ContainsField ("Digital Outputs"))
   xmppControlClient.Set (Jid, "Digital Outputs", i);
```

Setting up our Boolean alarm State parameter is done in the following manner:

```
if (b.HasValue && xmppControlForm.ContainsField ("State"))
   xmppControlClient.Set (Jid, "State", b.Value);
```

## Setting up a camera client interface

To emulate the UPnP event subscription model in XMPP, we converted our camera to a sensor. For our purposes, we need to subscribe to the camera image URL field property, together with its corresponding `Width` and `Height` field properties, when we initialize our camera interface. We do this in the same way as for the sensor, except that here we use another sequence number (-2) to keep the two apart, as mentioned in the next code:

```
private static void InitCamera (string Jid)
{
  xmppSensorClient.SubscribeData (-2, Jid, ReadoutType.Identity,
    null,new FieldCondition[]
  {
    FieldCondition.Report ("URL"),
      FieldCondition.IfChanged ("Width", 1),
      FieldCondition.IfChanged ("Height", 1)
  },
  null, null, new Duration (0, 0, 0, 0, 1, 0), true,
    string.Empty, string.Empty, string.Empty,
    NewCameraData, null);
}
```

Parsing this data is also done in the same way as we did in the sensor project.

## Fetching the camera image over XMPP

The URL provided by the camera will differ from the URL provided over normal UPnP in that it will use the `httpx` URI scheme. In our case, the URL to the camera image will be something like `httpx://camera.learningiot@thingk.me/camera`. In order to be able to use the `httpx` URI scheme, we have to tell the framework which XMPP client to use. This is done by registering it with the `HttpxUriScheme` class, which is defined in the `Clayster.Library.Internet.URIs` namespace, as follows:

```
HttpxUriScheme.Register (xmppClient);
```

Once the XMPP client has been registered, the system will treat the `httpx` URI scheme as it would treat any other registered URI scheme, such as the `http` and `https` URI schemes. We get the image by calling the static `HttpSocketClient.GetResource` method with the URL, and it will figure out what to do. We embed the content of the response, as we did with the images that were fetched using UPnP:

```
Response = HttpSocketClient.GetResource(Url);
Msg.EmbedObject ("cam1img" + j.ToString (),
  Response.Header.ContentType, Response.Data);
```

# Identifying peer capabilities

When things connect to the controller, they need to figure out what they can do, or what interoperability contracts they can publish so we can know what they are. As there is an interoperability server class, there is also an interoperability client class, as shown in the following code, that we can use for this purpose:

```
xmppInteroperabilityClient = new XmppInteroperabilityClient (
  xmppClient);
```

We will create a method that will be used to figure out what is behind a specific Jid by requesting its interoperability interfaces or contracts, as follows:

```
private static void CheckInterfaces (string Jid)
{
  xmppInteroperabilityClient.RequestInterfaces (Jid,
    (Interfaces, State) =>
    {
      ...
      xmppSettings.UpdateIfModified ();
    }, Jid);
}
```

The ellipsis ("…") in the preceding code corresponds to the different checks we do on the list of interfaces reported by the device. If we are not already connected to a sensor and a new thing with the corresponding light and motion interfaces are available, we remember the Jid (which is available in the State parameter as shown in the next code) for use as the sensor in our application:

```
if (string.IsNullOrEmpty (xmppSettings.Sensor) &&
  Array.IndexOf<string> (Interfaces,
  "Clayster.LearningIoT.Sensor.Light") >= 0 &&
  Array.IndexOf<string> (Interfaces,
  "Clayster.LearningIoT.Sensor.Motion") >= 0)
{
  xmppSettings.Sensor = (string)State;
  InitSensor (xmppSettings.Sensor);
}
```

In the same way, the actuator and camera are identified in a similar manner.

# Reacting to peer presence

Now that we have a method to identify what peers are, we need to trigger the method somehow. To be able to communicate with a peer, we will need the full JID, not just the bare JID, which we have when negotiating friendship relationships. The full JID requires the reception of a presence message from the device, showing it is online. To avoid triggering the method every time a device goes online, we first keep an internal list of peers that have been newly accepted as friends. This can be done with the following code:

```
Dictionary<string,bool> NewlyAdded =
  new Dictionary<string, bool> ();
```

In the `OnPresenceReceived` event handler, when a `Subscribed` presence stanza has been received, confirming a new friendship, we store away the bare JID in the list, as follows:

```
case PresenceType.Subscribed:
  lock (NewlyAdded)
  {
    NewlyAdded [XmppClient.StripResource (
    Presence.From).ToLower ()] = true;
  }
  break;
```

As shown in the next code snippet, we also add a `default` clause to catch presence stanzas of types other than `Subscribe`, `Subscribed`, `Unsubscribe`, and `Unsubscribed`. If not offline, we will consider that the peer is about to go online:

```
default:
  string s = XmppClient.StripResource
    (Presence.From).ToLower ();
  if (Presence.Status != PresenceStatus.Offline)
  {
```

First we need to check whether the device corresponds to a device the controller already uses. If this is the case, we need to reinitialize our subscriptions and get a new control form from the actuator since these might have been changed while offline. This can be done with the following code:

```
if (!string.IsNullOrEmpty (xmppSettings.Sensor) &&
  XmppClient.CompareJid (xmppSettings.Sensor, Presence.From))
    InitSensor (Presence.From);
else if (!string.IsNullOrEmpty (xmppSettings.Actuator) &&
  XmppClient.CompareJid (xmppSettings.Actuator, Presence.From))
    InitActuator (Presence.From);
```

```
      else if (!string.IsNullOrEmpty (xmppSettings.Camera) &&
        XmppClient.CompareJid (xmppSettings.Camera, Presence.From))
          InitCamera (Presence.From);
```

If not an already known device, we check whether we need to have a look at the capabilities at all with the following code. If the controller has already identified the devices it uses, it doesn't need to analyze new friends:

```
      else if (string.IsNullOrEmpty (xmppSettings.Sensor) ||
         string.IsNullOrEmpty (xmppSettings.Actuator) ||
         string.IsNullOrEmpty (xmppSettings.Camera))
      {
        lock (NewlyAdded)
        {
          if (!NewlyAdded.ContainsKey (s))
            break;
          NewlyAdded.Remove (s);
        }
        CheckInterfaces (Presence.From);
      }
    }
    break;
```

## Detecting rule changes

If the owner of a thing involved in a network changes the rules, it will ask the corresponding devices involved in the rule to clear their provisioning caches. This cache locally stores responses to previous provisioning questions, which might now be incorrect. The clearing of the cache is handled by our provisioning server class. But we can add an event handler to the `OnClearCache` event, which is raised whenever the cache is cleared, to reinitialize our connections, including event subscriptions and control forms. This event makes sure that the new rules that apply are taken into account. The following code is used in order to reinitialize our connections:

```
    xmppProvisioningServer.OnClearCache += (Sender, e) =>
    {
      if (!string.IsNullOrEmpty (xmppSettings.Sensor))
        InitSensor (xmppSettings.Sensor);
      if (!string.IsNullOrEmpty (xmppSettings.Actuator))
        InitActuator (xmppSettings.Actuator);
      if (!string.IsNullOrEmpty (xmppSettings.Camera))
        InitCamera (xmppSettings.Camera);
    };
```

# Connecting it all together

The XMPP implementation is now done. To access the complete source code, please download the example projects.

Since we have used a generic security model, based on identity creation and delegated trust to a provisioning server, our devices do not know who their owners are or with whom they can connect and communicate. To make everything work, we need to provide this information to the devices through the provisioning server. You can do this in the following way if you use the provisioning server at http://thingk.me/:

1. First, create an account on the **Dashboard** page.
2. Download a smart phone app to register your devices. This app is called Registration Unit or Thing Registrar. You can find the relevant instructions on the **API** page.
3. Run the app and create an XMPP account somewhere. You can use the XMPP server at thingk.me. This JID will be used when claiming ownership of the devices that would use the app. The JIDs will be reported to the corresponding devices, as the owner's JID.
4. On the **Registration** page, you can add your registration unit. This connects the app with the account. When adding a registration unit, you need to provide its JID. The server will send a message with a PIN code to your app to verify you have the right to use that JID. You need to confirm the receipt of this PIN code before you accept the unit as yours. You can use multiple registration units for each account.
5. From the app, you can now claim your things by taking photographs of their corresponding QR code. A list of claimed things will be shown on the **Things** page.
6. As soon as something new happens to your things, such as new friendship requests, readout requests, or control requests, the provisioning server will automatically recommend the thing to reject the corresponding request. But it will also notify you of the corresponding event. The **Dashboard** page will show any events you have pending, or send you an e-mail if you're not online. Follow the instructions in each notification and tell the server how you want it to respond the next time a similar request is made.
7. From the **Things** page, you can access all the information about each thing, reset and edit rules, recommend friendships, and also try to read and control them. It is from this page that you can connect the controller with the sensor, actuator, and camera by recommending new friendships to the controller.

8. You can connect normal chat clients to all your things as well. All devices have chat interfaces, so make sure to try this out.

9. You're welcome to contact `thingk.me` through the **Contact** page.

# Summary

In this chapter, we covered the basics of the XMPP protocol and some of its strengths and weaknesses. We saw how we can use it in our sensor, actuator, and controller projects as a simple means to create IoT applications. We also used the flexibility of the XMPP protocol to add an additional layer of security to each project using the pattern of delegated trust.

This chapter concludes with an overview of the different protocols used in IoT. For a comprehensive comparison between the protocols, listing features and perceived strengths and weaknesses of each in a table format, please refer to the paper *Biotic - Executive Summary* at `http://biotic-community.tumblr.com/`.

In the next chapter, we will introduce you to the use of platforms for IoT, and what additional features they provide when developing applications for IoT.

# Using an IoT Service Platform

In the previous chapters of this book, we studied various communication protocols that are suitable for use in **Internet of Things (IoT)**. So far, all our applications have been self-contained, and we have explicitly developed all the interfaces that are required for the applications to work. In this chapter, we will look at the benefits of using a service platform for IoT when we build services. Not only will it provide us with a suitable architecture and hardware abstraction model suitable for communication over a wide variety of protocols, it will also provide us with tools and interfaces to quickly host, administer, and monitor our services. It will also help us with a wide array of different development tasks making service development for the IoT much quicker and easier by removing or reducing repetitive tasks. By using a service platform, an IoT service developer can focus more of their time and energy on the development of the application logic itself. Thus, they can focus on development that will generate value.

In this chapter, you will learn:

- How to download and install the Clayster IoT service platform
- How to create, run and, debug a Clayster service
- How to use the Clayster Management Tool
- How to use existing XMPP architecture to facilitate development
- How to create 10-foot interface applications that display the state of the controller in real time

All the source code presented in this book is available for download. Source code for this chapter and the next one can be downloaded from `https://github.com/Clayster/Learning-IoT-IoTPlatform`.

# Selecting an IoT platform

There are many available platforms that developers can download and use. They vary greatly in functionality and development support. To get an idea of available platforms for IoT and M2M, you can go to `http://postscapes.com/internet-of-things-platforms` and review the registered platforms. You can then go to their corresponding web pages to learn more about what each platform can do.

Unfortunately, there's neither a way to easily compare platforms nor a comprehensive way to classify their features. In this chapter, we will use the Clayster IoT platform. It will help us with a lot of important tasks, which you will see in this chapter and the next. This will enable you to better assess what IoT platform to use and what to expect when you select one for your IoT projects.

# The Clayster platform

In this chapter, we will redevelop the Controller application that we developed in the previous chapter and call it Controller2. We will, however, develop it as a service to be run on the Clayster Internet of Things platform. In this way, we can compare the work that was required to develop it as a standalone application with the effort that is required to create it as a service running on an IoT platform. We can also compare the results and see what additional benefits we will receive by running our service in an environment where much that is required for a final product already exists.

# Downloading the Clayster platform

We will start the download of the Clayster platform by downloading its version meant for private use from `http://www.clayster.com/downloads`.

Before you are able to download the platform, the page will ask you to fill in a few personal details and a working e-mail address. When the form is filled, an e-mail will be sent to you to confirm the address. Once the e-mail address has been confirmed, a distribution of the platform will be built for you, which will contain your personal information. When this is done, a second e-mail will be sent to you that will contain a link to the distribution along with instructions on how to install it on different operating systems.

>  In our examples available for download, we have assumed that you will install Clayster platform on a Windows machine in the `C:\Downloads\ClaysterSmall` folder. This is not a requirement. If you install it in another folder or on another operating system, you might have to update the references to Clayster Libraries in the source code for the code to compile.

All the information about Clayster, including examples and tutorials, is available in a wiki. You can access this wiki at `https://wiki.clayster.com/`.

## Creating a service project

Creating a service project differs a little from how we created projects in the previous chapters. *Appendix A, Console Applications* outlines the process to create a simple console application. When we create a service for a service platform, the executable EXE file already exists. Therefore, we have to create a library project instead and make sure that the target framework corresponds to the version of the Clayster distribution (.NET 3.5 at the time of writing this book). Such a project will generate a **dynamic link library** (**DLL**) file. During startup, the Clayster executable file will load any DLL file it finds marked as a *Clayster Module* in its installation folder or any of its subfolders.

## Adding references

The Clayster distribution and runtime environment already contains all Clayster libraries. When we add references to these libraries from our project, we must make sure to use the libraries available in the Clayster distribution from the installation folder, instead of using the libraries that we used previously in this book. This will ensure that the project uses the correct libraries. Apart from the libraries used previously, there are a few new libraries available in the Clayster distribution that are new to us, and which we will need:

- `Clayster.AppServer.Infrastructure`: This library contains the application engine available in the platform. Apart from managing applications, it also provides report tools, cluster support, management support for operators and administrators; it manages backups, imports, exports, localization and various data sources used in IoT, and it also provides rendering support for different types of GUIs, among other things.

- `Clayster.Library.Abstract`: This library contains a data abstraction layer, and is a crucial tool for the efficient management of objects in the system.

- `Clayster.Library.Installation`: This library defines the concept of packages.

- `Clayster.Library.Meters`: This library replaces the `Clayster.Library.IoT` library used in previous chapters. It contains an abstraction model for things such as sensors, actuators, controllers, meters, and so on.

Apart from the libraries, we will also add two additional references to the project—this time to two service modules available in the distribution, which are as follows:

- `Clayster.HomeApp.MomentaryValues`: This is a simple service that displays momentary values using gauges. We will use this project to display gauges of our sensor values.
- `Clayster.Metering.Xmpp`: This module contains an implementation of XMPP on top of the abstraction model defined in the `Clayster.Library.Metersz` namespace. It does everything we did in the previous chapter and more.

## Making a Clayster module

Not all DLLs will be loaded by Clayster. It will only load the DLLs that are marked as Clayster modules. There are three requirements for a DLL to be considered as a Clayster module:

- The module must be CLS-compliant.
- It must be marked as a Clayster module.
- It must contain a public certificate with information about the developer.

> There are a lot of online services that allow you to create simple self-signed certificates. One such service can be found at www.getacert.com.

All these things can be accomplished through the `AssemblyInfo.cs` file, available in each .NET project. Enforcing CLS compliance is easy. All you need to do is add the `CLSCompliant` assembly attribute, defined in the `System` namespace, as follows:

```
using System;
[assembly: CLSCompliant(true)]
```

This will make sure that the compiler creates warnings every time it finds a construct that is not CLS-compliant.

The two last items can be obtained by adding a public (possibly self-generated) certificate as an embedded resource to the project and referencing it using the `Certificate` assembly attribute, defined in the `Clayster.Library.Installation` library, as follows:

```
[assembly: Certificate("LearningIoT.cer")]
```

>  This certificate is not used for identification or security reasons. Since it is embedded into the code, it is simple to extract. It is only used as a means to mark the module as a Clayster module and provide information about the developer, so that module-specific data is stored appropriately and locally in an intuitive folder structure.

## Executing the service

There are different ways in which you can execute a service. In a commercial installation, a service can be hosted by different types of hosts such as a web server host, a Windows service host or a standalone executable host. While the first two types are simpler to monitor and maintain in a production environment, the latter is much easier to work with during development. The service can also be hosted in a cluster of servers.

The small Clayster distribution you've downloaded contains a slightly smaller version of the standalone executable host that can be run on Mono. It is executed in a terminal window and displays logged events. It loads any Clayster modules found in its folder or any of its subfolders. If you copy the resulting DLL file to the Clayster installation folder, you can simply execute the service by starting the standalone server from Windows, as follows:

```
Clayster.AppServer.Mono.Standalone
```

If you run the application from Linux, you can execute it as follows:

```
$ sudo mono Clayster.AppServer.Mono.Standalone.exe
```

## Using a package manifest

Instead of manually copying the service file and any other associated project files, such as content files, the developer can create a package manifest file describing the files included in the package. This makes the package easier to install and distribute. In our example, we only have one application file, and so our manifest file becomes particularly simple to write. We will create a new file and call it `Controller2.packagemanifest`. We will write the following into this new file and make sure that it is marked as a content file:

```
<?xml version="1.0" encoding="utf-8" ?>
<ServicePackageManifest
xmlns="http://clayster.com/schema/ServicePackageManifest/v1.xsd">
  <ApplicationFiles>
    <ApplicationFile file="Controller2.dll"/>
```

```
            </ApplicationFiles>
</ServicePackageManifest>
```

 You can find more information on how to write package manifest file can be found at `https://wiki.clayster.com/mediawiki/index.php?title=Service_Package_Manifest_File`.

Now that we have a package manifest file, we can install the package and execute the standalone server from the command line in one go. For a Windows system we can use the following command:

```
Clayster.AppServer.Mono.Standalone -i Controller2.packagemanifest
```

On a Linux system the standalone server can be executed using the following command:

```
$ sudo mono Clayster.AppServer.Mono.Standalone.exe -i
  Controller2.packagemanifest
```

Before loading the server and executing the particular service, the executable file analyzes the package manifest file and copies all the files to the location where they belong.

# Executing from Visual Studio

If you are working with the professional version of Visual Studio, you can execute the service directly from the IDE. This will allow you to debug the code directly from the IDE. To do this, you need to open the properties by right-clicking on the project in the **Solution Explorer** and go to the **Debug** tab. As a **Start Action**, choose the **Start external program** option. There you need to search for the `Clayster.AppServer.Mono.Standalone.exe` file and enter `-i Controller2.packagemanifest` on the command line arguments box. Now you can execute and debug the service directly from the IDE.

# Configuring the Clayster system

The Clayster system does many things automatically for us that we have manually done earlier. For instance, it maintains a local object database, configures a web server, configures mail settings, connects to an XMPP server, creates an account, registers with a Thing Registry and provisioning server, and so on. However, we need to provide some details manually for this to work. We will do this by editing the `Clayster.AppServer.Infrastructure.Settings.xml` file.

In Raspberry Pi, we will do this with the following command:

```
$ sudo nano Clayster.AppServer.Infrastructure.Settings.xml
```

The file structure is already defined. All we need to do is provide values for the `SmtpSettings` element so that the system can send e-mails. We can also take this opportunity to validate our choice of XMPP server in the `XmppServerSettings` element, which by default is set to `thingk.me`, and our HTTP server settings, which are stored in the `HttpServerSettings` and `HttpCacheSettings` elements.

> You can find more detailed information about how to set up the system at `https://wiki.clayster.com/mediawiki/index.php?title=Clayster_Setting_Up_Index`.

## Using the management tool

Clayster comes with a management tool that helps you to manage the server. This **Clayster Management Tool** (**CMT**), can also be downloaded from `http://www.clayster.com/downloads`.

Apart from the settings file described in the previous section, all other settings are available from the CMT. This includes data sources, objects in the object database, current activities, statistics and reports, and data in readable event logs.

When the CMT starts, it will prompt you for connection details. Enter a name for your connection and provide the IP address of your Raspberry Pi (or `localhost` if it is running on your local machine). The default user name is `Admin`, and the default password is the blank password. Default port numbers will also be provided.

> To avoid using blank passwords, the CMT will ask you to change the password after the first login.

A typical login window that appears when CMT starts will looks like the following screenshot:

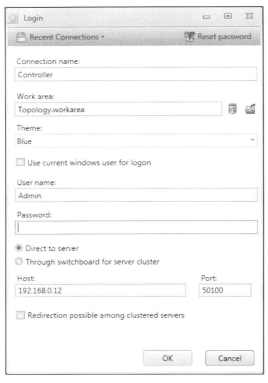

Login window in CMT

## Browsing data sources

Most of the configurable data in Clayster is ordered into data sources. These can be either tree-structured, flat or singular data sources. Singular data sources contain only one object. Flat data sources contain a list (ordered or unordered) of objects. Tree structured data sources contain a tree structure of objects, where each object in the structure represents a node. The tree-structured data sources are the most common, and they are also often stored as XML files. Objects in such data sources can be edited directly in the corresponding XML file, or indirectly through the CMT, other applications or any of the other available APIs.

When you open the CMT for the first time, make sure that you open the `Topology` data source. It is a tree-structured data source whose nodes represent IoT devices. The tree structure shows how they are connected to the system. The **Root** represents the server itself.

In the following example, we can see the system (**Root**) connected to an XMPP Server (via an account). Through this account, five entities can be accessed (as "friends"). Our sensor, actuator, and camera are available and online (marked in green). Our thing registrar app is a connection, but is not currently online. We are also connected to a Thing Registry and provisioning service. Each node adds its functionality to the system.

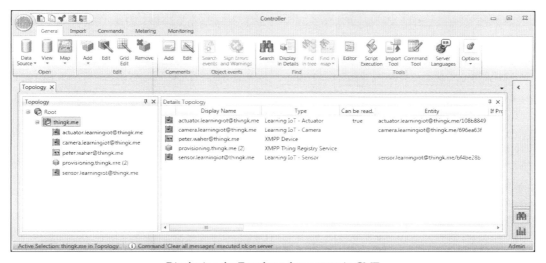

Displaying the Topology data source in CMT

In the CMT, you can view, modify, delete, import, and export all objects in these data sources. Apart from the `Topology` data source, there are a lot of other available data sources. Make sure that you familiarize yourself with them.

# Interfacing our devices using XMPP

XMPP is already implemented and supported through the `Clayster.Metering.Xmpp` module that we mentioned earlier. This module models each entity in XMPP as a separate node in the `Topology` data source. Connections with provisioning servers and thing registries are handled automatically through separate nodes dedicated to this task. Friendships are handled through simple child creation and removal operations. It can be done automatically through requests made by others or recommendations from the provisioning server, or manually by adding friends in the CMT. All we need to do is provide specialized classes that override base class functionality, and add specific features that are needed.

# Creating a class for our sensor

In our project, we will create a class for managing our sensor. We will derive it from the `XmppSensor` class defined in `Clayster.Metering.Xmpp` and provide the required default constructor through the following code:

```
public class Sensor : XmppSensor
{
  public Sensor()
  {
  }
}
```

Each class managed by `Clayster.Library.Abstract`, such as those used by the `Topology` data source, must define a `TagName` and a `Namespace` property. These are used during import and export to identify the class in question as follows:

```
public override string TagName
{
  get { return "IoTSensor"; }
}

public override string Namespace
{
  get { return "http://www.clayster.com/learningiot/"; }
}
```

We must also provide a human readable name to the class. Whenever objects of this class are displayed, for instance in the CMT, it is this human readable name that will be displayed, as shown in the following code:

```
public override string GetDisplayableTypeName
   (Language UserLanguage)
{
  return "Learning IoT - Sensor";
}
```

# Finding the best class

When the system finds a new device, it needs to know which class best represents that device. This is done by forcing each XMPP device class to implement a `Supports` method that returns to which degree the class handles said device, based on features and interoperability interfaces reported by the device. The class with the highest support grade is then picked to handle the newly found device.

By using the following code, we will override this method to provide a perfect match when our sensor is found:

```
public override SupportGrade Supports (
  XmppDeviceInformation DeviceInformation)
{
  if (Array.IndexOf<string> (
    DeviceInformation.InteroperabilityInterfaces,
    "Clayster.LearningIoT.Sensor.Light") >= 0 &&
    Array.IndexOf<string> (
    DeviceInformation.InteroperabilityInterfaces,
    "Clayster.LearningIoT.Sensor.Motion") >= 0)
    {
    return SupportGrade.Perfect;
    }
  else
    return SupportGrade.NotAtAll;
}
```

## Subscribing to sensor data

Manual readout of the sensor is already supported by the XmppSensor class. This means you can already read data from the sensor from the CMT, for instance, as it is. However, this is not sufficient for our application. We want to subscribe to the data from the sensor. This subscription is application-specific, and therefore must be done by us in our application. We will send a new subscription every time the sensor reports an online or chat presence. The XmppSensor class will then make sure that the subscription is sent again if the data is not received accordingly. The subscription call is similar to the one we did in the previous chapter. The subscription call is sent using the following code:

```
protected override void OnPresenceChanged (XmppPresence Presence)
{
  if (Presence.Status == PresenceStatus.Online ||
  Presence.Status == PresenceStatus.Chat)
  {
    this.SubscribeData (-1, ReadoutType.MomentaryValues,
      new FieldCondition[] {
        FieldCondition.IfChanged ("Temperature", 0.5),
        FieldCondition.IfChanged ("Light", 1),
        FieldCondition.IfChanged ("Motion", 1)
      }, null, null, new Duration (0, 0, 0, 0, 1, 0), true,
    this.NewSensorData, null);
  }
}
```

# Interpreting incoming sensor data

Interpreting incoming sensor data is done using the Clayster platform in a way that is similar to what we did using the `Clayster.Library.IoT` library in the previous chapters. We will start by looping through incoming fields:

```
private void NewSensorData (object Sender, SensorDataEventArgs e)
{
  FieldNumeric Num;
  FieldBoolean Bool;
  double? LightPercent = null;
  bool? Motion = null;

  if(e.HasRecentFields)
  {
    foreach(Field Field in e.RecentFields)
    {
      switch(Field.FieldName)
      {
```

There is one added advantage of handling field values when we run them on the Clayster platform: we can do unit conversions very easily. We will illustrate this with the help of an example, where we handle the incoming field value - temperature. First, we will try to convert it to Celsius. If successful, we will report it to our controller application (that will soon be created):

```
case "Temperature":
  if ((Num = Field as FieldNumeric) != null)
  {
    Num = Num.Convert ("C");
    if (Num.Unit == "C")
    Controller.SetTemperature (Num.Value);
  }
  break;
```

> There is a data source dedicated to unit conversion. You can create your own unit categories and units and determine how these relate to a reference unit plane, which is defined for each unit category. Unit conversions must be linear transformations from this reference unit plane.

We will handle the `Light` and `Motion` values in a similar way. Finally, after all the fields have been processed, we will call the Controller application and ask it to check its control rules:

```
if (LightPercent.HasValue && Motion.HasValue)
  Controller.CheckControlRules (
```

```
      LightPercent.Value, Motion.Value);
   }
}
```

Our `Sensor` class will then be complete.

# Creating a class for our actuator

If implementing support for our `Sensor` class was simple, implementing a class for our actuator is even simpler. Most of the actuator is already configured by the `XmppActuator` class. So, we will first create an `Actuator` class that is derived from this `XmppActuator` class. We will provide it with a `TagName` that will return `"IoTActuator"` and the same namespace that the `Sensor` class returns. We will use `Learning IoT - Actuator` as a displayable type name. We will also override the `Supports` method to return a perfect response when the corresponding interoperability interfaces are found.

## Customizing control operations

Our `Actuator` class is basically complete. The `XmppActuator` class already has support for reading out the control form and publishing the available control parameters. This can be tested in the CMT, for instance, where the administrator configures control parameters accordingly.

To make control of the actuator a bit simpler, we will add customized control methods to our class. We already know that the parameters exist (or should exist) since the corresponding interoperability interfaces (contracts) are supported.

We will begin by adding a method to update the LEDs on the actuator:

```
public void UpdateLeds(int LedMask)
{
   this.RequestConfiguration ((NodeConfigurationMethod)null,
      "R_Digital Outputs", LedMask, this.Id);
}
```

The `RequestConfiguration` method is called to perform a configuration. This method is defined by `Clayster.Library.Meters` namespace, and can be called for all configurable nodes in the system. Configuration is then performed from a context that is defined by the node. The `XmppActuator` class translates this configuration into the corresponding set operation, based on the data type of the parameter value.

The first parameter contains an optional callback method that is called after the parameter has been successfully (or unsuccessfully) configured. We don't require a callback, so we will only send a null parameter value. The second parameter contains the name of the parameter that needs to be configured. Local configurable parameters of the `XmppActuator` class differ from its remote configurable parameters, which are prefixed by `R_`. The third parameter value is the value that needs to be configured. The type of value to send here depends on the parameter used. The fourth and last parameter is a subject string that will be used when the corresponding configuration event is logged in the event log.

 You can find out which configurable parameters are available on a node by using the CMT.

In a similar fashion, we will add a method for controlling the alarm state of the actuator and then our `Actuator` class will be complete.

## Creating a class for our camera

In essence, our `Camera` class does not differ much from our `Sensor` class. It will only have different property values as well as a somewhat different sensor data subscription and field-parsing method. Interested readers can refer to the source code for this chapter.

## Creating our control application

We are now ready to build our control application. You can build various different kinds of applications on Clayster. Some of these have been listed as follows:

- **10-foot interface applications**: These applications are suitable for TVs, smart phones and tablets. They are created by deriving from the `Clayster.AppServer.Infrastructure.Application` class. The name emerged from the requirement that the application should be usable from a distance of 10 feet (about 3 meters), like a television set. This, for instance, requires large fonts and buttons, and no windows. The same interface design is suitable for all kinds of touch displays and smart phones.

- **Web applications**: These applications are suitable for display in a browser. These are created by deriving from the `Clayster.AppServer.Infrastructure.WebApplication` class. The `thingk.me` service is a web application running on the Clayster platform.

- **Non-visible services**: These services can be implemented, by the `Clayster.Library.Installation.Interfaces.IPluggableModule` interface.
- **Custom views:** These views for integration with the CMT can be implemented by deriving from `Clayster.Library.Layout.CustomView`.

The first two kinds of applications differ in one important regard: Web applications are assumed to be scrollable from the start, while 10-foot interface applications have to adhere to a fixed-size screen.

# Understanding rendering

When creating user interfaces in Clayster, the platform helps the developer by providing them with a powerful rendering engine. Instead of you having to provide a complete end user GUI with client-side code, the rendering engine creates one for you dynamically. Furthermore, the generated GUI will be created for the client currently being used by the user. The rendering engine only takes metadata about the GUI from the application and generates the GUI for the client. In this way, it provides a protective, generative layer between application logic and the end user client in much the same way as the object database handles database communication for the application, by using metadata available in the class definitions of objects that are being persisted.

The rendering pipeline can be simplistically described as follows:

1. The client connects to the server.
2. An appropriate renderer is selected for the client, based on protocol used to connect to the server and the capabilities of the client. The renderer is selected from a list of available renderers, which themselves are, to a large extent, also pluggable modules.
3. The system provides a Macro-layout for the client. This Macro-layout is devoid of client-specific details and resolutions. Instead, it consists of a basic subdivision of available space. Macro-layouts can also be provided as pluggable modules. In the leaf nodes of this Macro-layout, references are made either explicitly or implicitly to services in the system. These services then provide a Micro-layout that is used to further subdivide the available space. Micro-layout also provides content for the corresponding area.

 More information about Macro-layout and Micro-layout can be found here https://wiki.clayster.com/mediawiki/index.php?title=Macro_Layout_and_Micro_Layout.

4. The system then provides a theme, which contains details of how the layout should be rendered. Themes can also be provided as pluggable modules.
5. The final interactive GUI is generated and sent to the client. This includes interaction logic and support for push notification.

## Defining the application class

Since we haven't created a 10-foot interface application in the previous chapters, we will create one in this chapter to illustrate how they work. We will start by defining the class:

```
public class Controller : Application
{
  public Controller ()
  {
  }
```

## Initializing the controller

Much of the application initialization that we did in the previous chapters has already been taken care of by the system for us. However, we will still need a reference to the object database and a reduced mail settings class. Initialization is best done by overriding the OnLoaded method:

```
internal static ObjectDatabase db;
internal static MailSettings mailSettings;

public override void OnLoaded ()
{
  db = DB.GetDatabaseProxy ("TheController");
  mailSettings = MailSettings.LoadSettings ();

  if (mailSettings == null)
  {
    mailSettings = new MailSettings ();
    mailSettings.From = "Enter address of sender here.";
    mailSettings.Recipient =
       "Enter recipient of alarm mails here.";
    mailSettings.SaveNew ();
  }
}
```

# Adding control rules

The control rules we define for the application will be the same as those used in previous chapters. The only difference here is that we don't need to keep track of the type or number of devices that are currently connected to the controller. We can simply ask the Topology data source to return all the items of a given type, as follows:

```
if (!lastAlarm.HasValue || lastAlarm.Value != Alarm)
{
  lastAlarm = Alarm;
  UpdateClients ();

  foreach (Actuator Actuator in Topology.Source.GetObjects(
    typeof(Actuator), User.AllPrivileges))
      Actuator.UpdateAlarm (Alarm);

  if (Alarm)
  {
    Thread T = new Thread (SendAlarmMail);
    T.Priority = ThreadPriority.BelowNormal;
    T.Name = "SendAlarmMail";
    T.Start ();
  }
}
```

The second parameter in the GetObjects call is a user object. It is possible to limit access to objects in a data source based on access privileges held by the role of the user. A predefined user having all access rights (User.AllPrivileges) assures us that we will get all the objects of the corresponding type. Also, note that we made a call to an UpdateClients method. We will define this method later. It will ensure that anything that causes changes in the GUI is pushed up to the connected end users.

> Users, roles, and privileges are three separate data sources that are available in Clayster. You can manage these in the CMT if you have sufficient privileges. Nodes in the Topology data source can require visible custom privileges. Edit the corresponding nodes to set such custom privileges. This might allow you to create an environment with compartmentalized access to Topology data source and other data sources.

# Understanding application references

Macro-layouts provided by the system can reference applications in the system in different ways:

- **Menu reference**: A menu reference consists of a reference to the application together with an instance name string. Micro-layout for a menu reference is fetched by calling the `OnShowMenu` method on the corresponding application. There are three types of menu references:
    - **Standard menu reference**: This appears in normal menus.
    - **Custom menu reference**: This is a custom area of custom size. It can be considered a widget. In Clayster, such a widget is called a brieflet.
    - **Dynamic selection reference**: This is a selection area that can display detailed information about a selected item from a selected application on the screen.

- **Dialog reference**: A dialog reference consists of a reference to an application, together with an instance name string and a dialog name string. Micro-layout for a dialog reference will be fetched by calling the `OnShowDialog` method on the corresponding application.

# Defining brieflets

In our example, we will only use custom menu references, or the so-called brieflets. We don't need to create menus for navigation or dialogs containing user interaction. Everything that we need to display will fit into one simple screen. First, we will tell the system that the application will not be visible in regular menus:

```
public override bool IsShownInMenu(IsShownInMenuEventArgs e)
{
   return false;
}
```

This is the method in which the application can publish standard menu references. We will then define the brieflets that we want to publish. This will be done by overriding the `GetBrieflets` method, as follows:

```
public override ApplicationBrieflet[] GetBrieflets (
   GetBriefletEventArgs e)
{
return new ApplicationBrieflet[] {
   new ApplicationBrieflet ("Temperature",
      "Learning IoT - Temperature", 2, 2),
   new ApplicationBrieflet ("Light",
```

```
          "Learning IoT - Light", 2, 2),
      new ApplicationBrieflet ("Motion",
          "Learning IoT - Motion", 1, 1),
      new ApplicationBrieflet ("Alarm",
          "Learning IoT - Alarm", 1, 1)
  };
}
```

The first parameter in each brieflet definition is the instance name identifying the brieflet. The second parameter is a human readable string that is used when a list of available brieflets is presented to a human user. The last two parameters correspond to the size of the brieflet. The unit that is used is the number of "squares" in an imaginary grid. A menu item in a touch menu can be seen as a 1 x 1 square.

## Displaying a gauge

All our brieflets are customized menu items. So, to display something in one of our brieflets, we just need to return the corresponding Micro-layout by overriding the `OnShowMenu` method. In this example, we want to start by returning Micro-layout for the temperature brieflet:

```
public override MicroLayout OnShowMenu (ShowEventArgs e)
{
   switch (e.InstanceName)
   {
     case "Temperature":
```

Micro-layout can be defined either by using XML or dynamically through code, where each XML element corresponds to a class with the same name. We will use the second approach since it is easier to create a dynamic Micro-layout this way. We will use the application `Clayster.HomeApp.MomentaryValues`, available in the distribution, to quickly draw a bitmap image containing a gauge displaying our sensor value. This is shown in the following code snippet:

```
MicroLayoutElement Value;
System.Drawing.Bitmap Bmp;

if (temperatureC.HasValue)
{
  Bmp = Clayster.HomeApp.MomentaryValues.Graphics.GetGauge
     (15, 25, temperatureC.Value, "°C", GaugeType.GreenToRed);
  Value = new ImageVariable (Bmp);
}
else
  Value = new Label ("N/A");
```

Using an IoT Service Platform

>  Bitmap content can be displayed using either `ImageVariable` or `ImageConstant` (or any of its descendants). We have used `ImageVariable` in this example and we will use `ImageConstant` to display camera images.
>
> Constant images also provide a string ID, which identifies the image. Using this ID, the image can be cached on the client, and it will be fetched from the server only if the client does not already have the image in its cache. This requires less communication resources, but may induce flicker when the image changes and the new image is not available in the cache and while it is being loaded. `ImageVariable` supposes the image to be new for every update. It requires more communication resources, but provides updates without flicker since the image data is embedded into the frame directly. You can try the two different methods separately to get a feel for how they work.

When we get the gauge—or the label if no value is available—we will return the Micro-layout. Remember that Macro-layout and Micro-layout work by subdividing the available space, rather than placing controls on a form. In our case, we will divide the available space into two rows of relative heights 1:3, the top one containing a header and the lower one the gauge or label:

```
return new MicroLayout (new Rows (
  new Row (1, HorizontalAlignment.Center,
    VerticalAlignment.Center,
    Paragraph.Header1 ("Temperature")),
  new Row (3, HorizontalAlignment.Center,
    VerticalAlignment.Center, Value)));
```

The brieflet showing the light gauge is handled in exactly the same way.

## Displaying a binary signal

The layouts for the binary motion and alarm signals are laid out in a manner similar to what we just saw, except the size of the brieflet is only 1 x 1:

```
case "Motion":
  Value = this.GetAlarmSymbol (motion);

  return new MicroLayout (new Rows (
    new Row (1, HorizontalAlignment.Center,
      VerticalAlignment.Center,
      Paragraph.Header1 ("Motion")),
```

```
            new Row (2, HorizontalAlignment.Center,
               VerticalAlignment.Center, Value)));
```

The same code is required for the alarm signal as well. A binary signal can be displayed by using two constant images. One represents 0 or the "off" state, and the other represents 1 or the "on" state. We will use this method in binary brieflets by utilizing two images that are available as embedded resources in the application `Clayster.HomeApp.MomentaryValues`, to illustrate the point:

```
private MicroLayoutElement GetAlarmSymbol(bool? Value)
{
   if (Value.HasValue)
   {
     if (Value.Value)
     {
       return new MicroLayout (new ImageMultiResolution (
         new ImageConstantResource (
            "Clayster.HomeApp.MomentaryValues." +
            "Graphics._60x60.Enabled." +
            "blaljus.png", 60, 60),
         new ImageConstantResource (
            "Clayster.HomeApp.MomentaryValues." +
            "Graphics._45x45.Enabled." +
            "blaljus.png", 45, 45)));
     }
     else
        return new MicroLayout (new ImageMultiResolution (
          new ImageConstantResource (
            "Clayster.HomeApp.MomentaryValues." +
            "Graphics._60x60.Disabled." +
            "blaljus.png", 60, 60),
          new ImageConstantResource (
            "Clayster.HomeApp.MomentaryValues." +
            "Graphics._45x45.Disabled." +
            "blaljus.png", 45, 45)));
   }
   else
   return new Label ("N/A");
}
```

Micro-layout supports the concept of multiresolution images. By providing various options, the renderer can choose the image that best suits the client, given the available space at the time of rendering.

# Pushing updates to the client

It's easy to push updates to a client. First, you need to enable such push notifications. This can be done by enabling events in the application as follows. By default, such events are disabled:

```
public override bool SendsEvents
get { return true; }
```

Each client is assigned a location. For web applications, this location is temporary. For 10-foot interfaces, it corresponds to a `Location` object in the geo-localized `Groups` data source. In both cases, each location has an object ID or `OID`. To forward changes to a client, an application will raise an event providing the `OID` corresponding to the location where the change should be executed. The system will handle the rest. It will calculate what areas of the display are affected, render a new layout and send it to the client.

> All areas of the screen corresponding to the application will be updated on the corresponding client. If you have multiple brieflets being updated asynchronously from each other, it is better to host these brieflets using different application classes in the same project. This avoids unnecessary client updates. In our code, we will divide our brieflets between three different applications, one for sensor values, one for camera images and one for test command buttons.

Push notifications in our application are simple. We want to update any client who views the application after a sensor value is updated, regardless of the location from which the client views the application. To do this, we first need to keep track of which clients are currently viewing our application. We define a `Dictionary` class as follows:

```
private static Dictionary<string,bool> activeLocations =
  new Dictionary<string, bool> ();
```

We will populate this `Dictionary` class with the object IDs `OID` of the location of the clients as they view the application:

```
public override void OnEventNotificationRequest
  (Location Location)
{
  lock(activeLocations)
  {
    activeLocations [Location.OID] = true;
  }
}
```

And depopulate it as soon as a client stops viewing the application:

```
public override void OnEventNotificationNoLongerRequested
  (Location Location)
{
  lock (activeLocations)
  {
    activeLocations.Remove (Location.OID);
  }
}
```

To get an array of locations that are currently viewing the application, we will simply copy the keys of this dictionary into an array that can be safely browsed:

```
public static string[] GetActiveLocations ()
{
  string[] Result;
  lock (activeLocations)
  {
  Result = new string[activeLocations.Count];
    activeLocations.Keys.CopyTo (Result, 0);
  }
  return Result;
}
```

Updating clients is now easy. Whenever a new sensor value is received, we will call the UpdateClients method, which in turn will register an event on the application for all clients currently viewing it. The platform will take care of the rest:

```
private static string appName = typeof(Controller).FullName;

private static void UpdateClients ()
{
  foreach (string OID in GetActiveLocations())
    EventManager.RegisterEvent (appName, OID);
}
```

## Completing the application

The source code for our project contains more brieflets that are defined in two more application classes. The CamStorage class contains three brieflets that show the last three camera images that were taken. They use ImageConstant to display the image to the client. The application also pushes updates to clients in the same way in which the Controller class does. However, by putting the brieflets in a separate application, we can avoid updating the entire screen when a new camera image is taken or when sensor values change.

*Using an IoT Service Platform*

A third application class named `TestApp` publishes two small brieflets, each containing a **Test** button that can be used to test the application. It becomes quickly apparent if the sensor is connected and works, since changes to sensor values are followed by changes in the corresponding gauges. To test the actuator, one brieflet publishes a **Test** button. By clicking on it, you can test the LED and alarm outputs. A second brieflet publishes a **Snapshot** button. By clicking this button you can take a photo, if a camera is connected, and update any visible camera brieflets.

## Configuring the application

We can now try the application. We will execute the application as described earlier. The first step is to configure the application so that the devices become friends and can interchange information with each other. This step is similar to what we did in the previous chapter. You can either configure friendships manually or use `thingk.me` to control access permissions between the different projects and the new service.

Note that the application will create a new *JID* for itself and register it with the provisioning server. It will also log a *QR* code to the event log, which will be displayed in the terminal window. This QR code can be used to claim ownership of the controller.

Remember to use the CMT application to monitor the internal state of your application when creating friendships and trying readouts and control operations. From the CMT, you can open line listeners to monitor actual communication. This can be done by right-clicking the node in the `Topology` data source that represents the XMPP server.

## Viewing the 10-foot interface application

After starting the Clayster platform with our service, we can choose various ways to view the application. We can either use a web browser or a special Clayster View application. For simplicity's sake, we'll use a web browser. If the IP address of our controller is `192.168.0.12`, we can view the 10-foot interface at `http://192.168.0.12/Default.ext?ResX=800&ResY=600&HTML5=1&MAC=000000000001&SimDisplay=0&SkipDelay=1`.

For a detailed description on how to form URLs for 10-foot interface clients, see `https://wiki.clayster.com/mediawiki/index.php?title=Startup_URLs`.

There are various ways to identify the location object to which the client corresponds. This identification can be done by using the client's IP address, MAC address, login user name, certificate thumbprint, XMPP address, or a combination of these.

>  The ClaysterSmall distribution comes with a Groups data source containing one location object identified by MAC address `000000000001`. If you are using other identification schemes, or a client that reports a true MAC address, then the corresponding location object must be updated. For more information on this go to `https://wiki.clayster.com/mediawiki/index.php?title=Groups_-_Location`.

You can also configure the system to automatically add Location objects to your Groups data source. This would allow automatic installation of new client devices.

To be able to configure the screen the way we want, we will enter the **Settings** menu, click on the **Layout** menu item and select the **No Menu 5x4** option. This will clear the display and allow you to experiment with placing brieflets over the entire screen using a 5x4 grid of squares. Simply click on the user-defined layout on an area that does not have a brieflet, and you can select which brieflet you want to display there.

After arranging the brieflets the way we want, the screen might look something like the following screenshot. Gauges, binary signals, and camera images will be automatically pushed to the client, and from this interface we can see both the current state of the controller as well as test all the parts of the system.

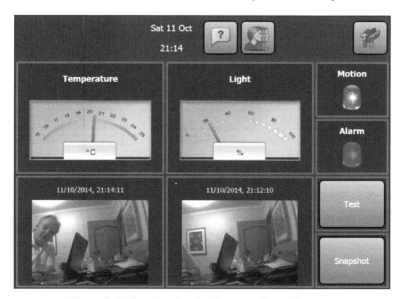

Example 10-foot interface for the controller application

The first time that a client connects to the server, immediately after the server has been restarted, the server might seem slow in its response. Don't worry. Managed code is compiled the first time it is executed. So, the first time a client connects, a lot of code will be **just in time (JIT)** compiled. Once JIT compilation is done, the application will execute much quicker. Such a JIT-compiled code will stay compiled until the server application is closed or the server is restarted.

# Summary

In this chapter, we introduced the concept of **IoT** service platforms and what they can be used for. **IoT** helps developers with common and required implementation tasks such as database communication, end user GUI generation, management, monitoring, administrative tasks, reporting, hosting, clustering, and so on. We saw the benefits of this approach by comparing the controller implementation on the Clayster platform with the controller implementation made in previous chapters.

In the next chapter, we will show you how the abstraction layers defined in such a platform can be used to efficiently create protocol gateways.

# 8
# Creating Protocol Gateways

In the previous chapter, we learned the benefits of creating applications using the **Internet of Things** (**IoT**) platform. In this chapter, we will show you how such a platform can be used to bridge different protocols so that devices and applications in different networks that use different protocols can communicate with each other. There may be many reasons why you would need to bridge between protocols in **IoT**. A few of them are listed here:

- To include services and devices to talk to other services and devices using other protocols if you're interconnecting systems
- To extend the reach of systems and networks to include areas where different protocols are required
- If you're building services using third-party devices
- If you're building devices that third-party services might want to use
- If you're creating an architecture for distributed and open networks for smart buildings or smart cities
- To allow interconnectivity of consumer electronics for **IoT**
- To enhance the overall interoperability on the Internet

In this chapter, you will learn:

- The benefits of using a good abstraction model for **IoT**
- How to integrate protocols into such an abstraction model
- How to bridge multiple protocols in real time using an abstraction model

We will show the basics of how the `Clayster.Meterig.CoAP` module was developed, which is available in the `ClaysterSmall` platform distribution and introduced in the previous chapter. We will do this in a parallel project called `CoapGateway` whose source code can be downloaded for free.

>  All of the source code presented in this book is available for download. Source code for this chapter and the next can be downloaded here:
> `https://github.com/Clayster/Learning-IoT-Gateway`

## Understanding protocol bridging

Consider the problem of creating a simple bridge between two protocols, say XMPP and CoAP introduced in the previous chapters. For a device that communicates through XMPP to be able to interact with a device that uses CoAP, a bridge needs to be inserted in between. This bridge would need to be able to translate requests made using XMPP to a request made using CoAP, then translate the CoAP response back to an XMPP response. In the same way, if a CoAP device wants to request something from an XMPP device, the bridge would need to translate the CoAP request into an XMPP request and then translate the XMPP response back to a CoAP response. It is easy to see we need a pair of translators from one protocol to the other and vice versa.

However, what happens if we want to introduce a third protocol, say MQTT, into the picture? In this case, three pairs of protocol translators would be required: CoAP and XMPP, MQTT and XMPP, and CoAP and MQTT. Another complexity arises with the introduction of MQTT. What happens when protocols do not support the same semantics? CoAP and XMPP support the request/response and event subscription patterns, while XMPP and MQTT support the publish/subscribe pattern. MQTT does not support the request/response and event subscription patterns. How should these differences be handled? One way to handle these patterns in MQTT is for the gateway to buffer the latest reported values and report them immediately if requested, as if the device had supported the corresponding patterns. Another important pattern not supported by MQTT is the point-to-point asynchronous messaging pattern.

Note that some patterns available for these different protocols might be similar, but not equal. The event subscription pattern, for instance, differs from the topic subscription pattern in that it allows clients to subscribe individually to events using individual event triggers. The topic subscription pattern does not support individual event triggers, and the subscribers will have to be contented with the triggers defined by the publisher regardless of the application.

If we want to handle four protocols by including HTTP support, we would need six different protocol translation pairs. Out of these, five protocols would require 10 protocol translation pairs, six protocols would require 15 pairs, seven would require 21 pairs, and so on. In general, if $N$ protocols are supported, $N(N - 1)/2$ protocol translation pairs would have to be supported. Each time you add support for a protocol, the work becomes more difficult. It is clear that this approach quickly becomes impractical and unsupportable. This can be understood well with the help of the following diagram:

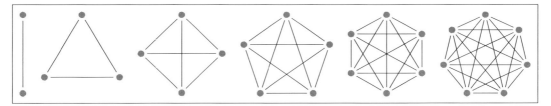

Protocol translation pairs grow as O(N2) without the abstraction model

# Using an abstraction model

It is quickly realized that building a protocol gateway by implementing translation pairs between protocols directly is very inefficient and difficult to maintain. A more fruitful path is to use a common abstraction model suitable for **IoT** and the translation of operations between different protocols. If such an abstraction model is used, translation pairs only need to translate between a given protocol and the abstraction model. This method is more efficient when it comes to implementation and quality assurance than direct translation if more than three different protocols are supported. While translating between two different protocols, you simply need to translate to the common abstraction model first and then use the second translation pair to translate from the abstraction model to the corresponding protocol.

Apart from shortening the development time drastically, a good abstraction model also helps in other ways. It can be used by internal services and administrative processes to administer and communicate with devices regardless of the protocol being used underneath. The `CoapGateway` project uses the abstraction model provided by the Clayster platform, which was introduced in the previous chapter. As such, it can be used to bridge the CoAP protocol with any other protocol hosted by the platform. Since the `ClaysterSmall` distribution already has support for XMPP through the `Clayster.Metering.Xmpp` module and MQTT through the `Clayster.Metering.Mqtt` module, our new `CoapGateway` project can be used to bridge the CoAP, XMPP, and MQTT protocols. This can be seen in the following diagram:

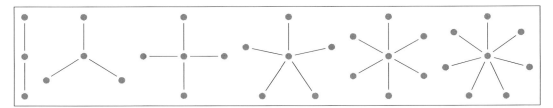

Protocol translation pairs grow as O(N) using an intermediary abstraction model

What is a good abstraction model? The challenging part is to create an abstraction model that is not too concrete. A concrete model might allow you to unknowingly paint yourself into a corner from where you would not be able to move later. This happens when you realize that you need to do something you've never done before, something that is not supported because the model is not sufficiently general. Another challenge is of course to avoid over-abstracting the model, which would make it difficult to use.

Abstraction models will be the point where **IoT** platforms will distinguish themselves over time. Which platform allows developers to do more over time, taking into consideration that it is not known today what will be developed in the future? Who can provide the most fruitful abstraction model for **IoT**?

The Clayster **IoT** platform is based on 20 years of experience in the fields of M2M and **IoT**; hence, its abstraction model has evolved over time and is easy to use, powerful, and supports a wide range of different use cases. By studying its abstraction model, you are better equipped to determine which platforms suits your long-term requirements.

# The basics of the Clayster abstraction model

To understand the implementation of the CoAP protocol bridge in the `CoapGateway` project, it's important to understand the abstraction model used by Clayster, defined in `Clayster.Library.Abstract`. To create a protocol bridge, we only need to implement the actual translation between CoAP operations and the abstraction model since the platform does the rest for us.

## Understanding editable data sources

In Clayster, you can store objects in the object database, as we have demonstrated earlier. But to manage large quantities of objects in a localized environment, you need to synchronize them across multiple clients and servers in a cluster, import and export them, and so on; this means that more than simple data persistence is required.

For this reason, the basic abstraction model in Clayster starts with a data abstraction model, which defines how configurable data is managed in the system. Data is stored in editable data sources, and each data source is derived from the `EditableDataSource` class. The keyword "editable" here means the contents can be managed dynamically from both services and management tools, as long as sufficient privileges are granted.

Most data sources in Clayster either store data in editable XML files (`EditableXmlFileDataSource`) or maintain data in only the memory (`EditableInMemoryDataSource`), even though developers can easily develop their own types of editable data sources if they wish to.

The system maintains a set of published data sources that can be managed by external tools and services (EditableDataSources). This set is ordered into a tree structure of data sources where each node references a data source (EditableDataSourceReference), as shown in the following diagram:

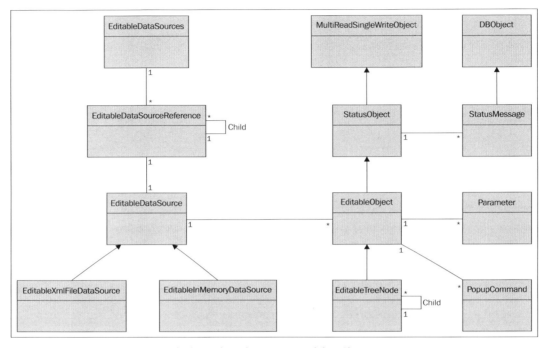

The basic data abstraction model in Clayster

## Understanding editable objects

Data in editable data sources comprises editable objects (EditableObject). If a data source contains a single object, it is said to be singular. Flat data sources contain a possibly ordered linear set of objects. However, most data sources contain objects structured into tree structures where each node in the tree is represented by a specialized version of the editable object (EditableTreeNode).

Each editable object is also a status object (StatusObject), an object that maintains a state and a set of status messages (StatusMessage) that are persisted in the object database (DBObject). These status messages can have different life cycles and levels and be of different types, such as informational, warning, error, and exception messages. They can be signed by different operators and are synchronized across the server cluster if available.

Each status object is also an object that can be used in a multithreaded and multiuser environment (`MultiReadSingleWriteObject`). Through methods in this class, editable objects can be safely managed in an environment where multiple services and users simultaneously work with them, without risking loss of data or inconsistent behavior.

Each editable object has two sets (possible empty) of parameters (`Parameter`) that control its behavior. One set is used to define the object behavior on the platform side. This set is referred to as the object properties. These properties are synchronized between all the clients and servers in the cluster. The second set is used to configure functionality in any underlying hardware or backend that corresponds to the object. This set is referred to as configurable parameters.

> There are many different types of parameters supported by the platform. Each one is managed by a separate class and derived from the `Parameter` class. They can be found in the `Clayster.Library.Abstract.ParameterTypes` namespace.

Editable objects can also publish a (possibly empty) set of pop-up commands of different types. There can be simple commands, parameterized commands, and parameterized queries. These context-sensitive commands as well as all the properties, configurable parameters, editable objects, and data sources are available in the management tools, such as **Clayster Management Tool** (**CMT**) introduced in the previous chapter, as long as user privileges permit them to.

## Using common data sources

Apart from developing services for Clayster, we can control Clayster's functionality by providing new classes of editable objects for existing data sources. This is particularly the case when creating protocol gateways. For this reason, we will provide a short introduction to some of the pre-existing data sources available in Clayster, which might come in handy. You might already be familiar with some of these sources from the previous chapter.

The `Users` data source contains `User` objects that correspond to user accounts that can log in to the system. Each user is assigned a role, represented by a `Role` object in the `Roles` data source. Each `Role` object in turn is assigned a set of privileges, and each privilege is represented by a `Privilege` object in the `Privileges` data source. This data source is formed as a tree structure of `Privilege` objects, making it possible for roles to be assigned with all the branches of privileges.

Everything related to communication with devices and processing of sensor data is organized into data sources in the `Metering` category. The `Topology` source contains all the devices and how they are connected. The `Unit Conversion` source contains all unit categories and corresponding units and information about how to convert between compatible units. The `Jobs` source contains jobs (for instance, readout or report jobs) that can be executed once or regularly. The `Groups` source allows the logical and geospatial structuring of devices, as opposed to the `Topology` source that specifies the physical connection structure. Sensor data (or Fields) can be processed by processors defined in the `Field Processors` data source. They can be stored or otherwise processed through field sinks defined in the `Field Sinks` data source. Fields can also be imported into the system through objects defined in the `Field Imports` data source.

## Overriding key properties and methods

While creating new editable object classes, you first need to choose an appropriate class to derive your new class from. Since most of the operational functionality is already provided by the platform, all you need to do is override some key properties and methods to provide the information the system needs to have in order to handle objects of the new class properly. You don't need to register created classes anywhere. It's sufficient to declare a class, and the system will automatically find it and be able to use it according to the information provided in these properties and methods.

Following is a brief description of a few central properties and methods that are of interest to us.

### Controlling structure

The `TagName` and `Namespace` properties are used during serialization and deserialization to identify the class that corresponds to the serialized object. The `GetDisplayableTypeName()` method can be used to provide a localized human-readable name for the class. The `GetIconResourceName()` method can be used to associate the class with one or more icons, depending on the object states. The `CanBeAddedTo()` and `CanTakeNewNode()` methods can be used to control where the objects of the corresponding class can appear in a tree structure.

## Publishing properties

Object properties are published and managed using a set of four methods. Implementing these four methods will automatically provide support for all the more advanced functions available in the system. These methods are only called when the object has been locked appropriately, corresponding to the operation being performed. So there is no need to worry about multiple threads accessing the object simultaneously in these methods. The GetParametersLocked() method is used to retrieve a set of available parameters. This set will contain sufficient localized metainformation about the properties to be able to provide the end users with a dialog to edit the properties. The GetParameterValueLocked() and SetParameterLocked() methods are used to get and set individual parameter values, while the GetParameterNamesLocked() method can be used to retrieve a list of the available property names.

## Publishing commands

All editable objects can publish commands that can be executed either manually or in automation operations. The GetPopupCommands() method returns a set of available commands on an object. Depending on the type of command, different methods are called to execute them. The simplest type of command, one that does not take any parameters, is executed through calls to the ExecuteSimplePopupCommand() method. All other commands require parameters. These parameters are returned from calls to the GetParametersForCommand() method. If it is a normal parameterized command, it is then executed by calling the ExecuteParameterPopupCommand() method.
A third type of command, a parameterized query, is executed through calls to the ExecuteParameterPopupQuery() method. These query commands return data to the client asynchronously. This data can be sequences of tabular data, images, or other types of objects.

## Handling communication with devices

The Topology data source contains a set of editable objects that are derived from the Node class defined in Clayster.Library.Meters. This class defines common properties and methods that are used to read and configure the corresponding devices.

## Reading devices

A node corresponds to a readable device if the `IsReadable` property returns *true*. If this is the case, anybody with the correct privileges can request to read the node. This is done by calling the `RequestReadout()` method. When it is time to read the node, the `ProcessReadoutRequest()` method is called. Who calls this method depends on the hierarchy of nodes in the topology. But it can be assumed a thread has been allocated somewhere if the readout is performed synchronously and that it is now processing the readout request. The corresponding node will be in a read state when this happens, which prohibits any changes to its properties.

## Configuring devices

If a device can be written to or configured, the `IsWritable` property should return true. If it is, anybody (with the corresponding privileges) can request to configure the node accordingly by calling the `RequestConfiguration()` method. A set of available configurable parameters is returned from the `GetConfigurableParametersLocked()` method. The `IsValidConfiguration()` method is called to check whether a corresponding parameter name and value pair is valid. Finally, when a parameter is to be written to the device, the `ProcessConfiguration()` method is called. As in the case of reading the device, the node will be in a read state when this call occurs, and depending on the node hierarchy, a thread will be allocated to execute the method accordingly.

# Understanding the CoAP gateway architecture

The `CoapGateway` architecture is simple and straightforward. The following illustration shows the available classes and their internal relationships. Classes that are colored off-white are defined in `Clayster.Library.Abstract`. The yellow/orange colored classes are defined in `Clayster.Library.Meters` and provide the basic functionality for the `Topology` data source. The blue classes are defined in `Clayster.Library.Internet`, and in our case, they provide us with communication capabilities. We have used these classes in our previous chapters. The green and pink classes are defined in our `CoapGateway` project. The color green represents structural nodes, while pink represents classes performing concrete work. All these classes are defined in the `.cs` files with the same name in the downloadable source code.

To add support for CoAP to the Clayster platform, you need to begin by adding a `CoapPort` object to the root of the topology. This object performs the actual communication and can also receive incoming requests. It uses a `CoapTopologyBridge` CoAP resource to publish the available nodes in the topology regardless of the protocol being used. Also, it is accessible by a user account that needs to be provided on the network using the CoAP protocol. This class translates CoAP requests to our common abstraction model and returns CoAP responses to these requests.

The other direction (sending CoAP requests and interpreting CoAP responses) is handled by the `CoapServer` class and any child nodes added to it. This class is added to the `CoapPort` class and is derived from `IpNode`, which provides an IP address and port number property. It is in turn derived from `ThreadNode`, which provides the execution context for the node and all its children. It also publishes a `Scan` command that can be evoked to scan the device for available resources. The architecture of the CoAP gateway is shown in the following diagram:

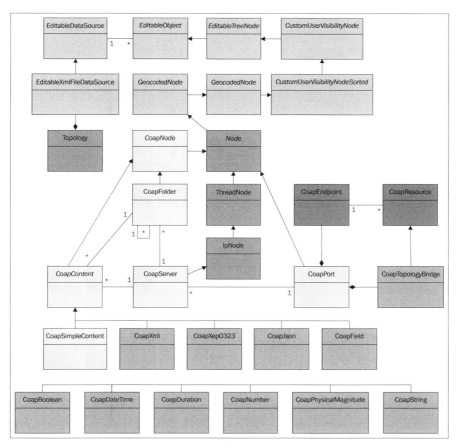

Architecture of the CoAP gateway project

Objects of the `CoapServer` class accept any number of `CoapFolder` objects as children. Both `CoapServer` and `CoapFolder` objects accept objects that are derived from `CoapContent`, which means they are resources that can be read. There are simple content resources that report a single data field and complex resources that report sets of fields. Here, you can add any type of class you want to handle different content types.

The existing classes provide a starting point and show how to perform such a translation. The following image shows how the topology can be ordered to read our CoAP sensor created in the *Chapter 4, The CoAP Protocol*. Since XMPP is supported by the server, all these devices will now automatically be available on the XMPP network as well. The other direction also holds true. Any XMPP devices available in the topology will be available using CoAP as well.

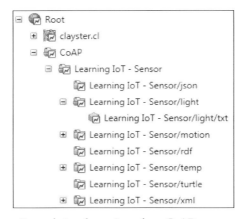

Example topology view of our CoAP sensor

# Summary

In this chapter, we introduced how the abstraction models in the **IoT** service platforms can be used to create protocol gateways. In the next and final chapter, we will discuss security and interoperability in **IoT**.

# 9
# Security and Interoperability

In the previous chapters, we experimented with a lot of different technologies that can be used for **Internet of Things** (**IoT**), but we did not delve into details about security and interoperability issues to any extent. In this chapter, we will focus on this topic and what issues we need to address during the design of the overall architecture to avoid many of the unnecessary problems that might otherwise arise and minimize the risk of painting yourself into a corner. You will learn the following:

- Risks with **IoT**
- Modes of attacking a system and some counter measures
- The importance of interoperability in **IoT**

## Understanding the risks

There are many solutions and products marketed today under the label **IoT** that lack basic security architectures. It is very easy for a knowledgeable person to take control of devices for malicious purposes. Not only devices at home are at risk, but cars, trains, airports, stores, ships, logistics applications, building automation, utility metering applications, industrial automation applications, health services, and so on, are also at risk because of the lack of security measures in their underlying architecture. It has gone so far that many western countries have identified the lack of security measures in automation applications as a risk to national security, and rightly so. It is just a matter of time before somebody is literally killed as a result of an attack by a hacker on some vulnerable equipment connected to the Internet. And what are the economic consequences for a company that rolls out a product for use on the Internet that results into something that is vulnerable to well-known attacks?

How has it come to this? After all the trouble Internet companies and applications have experienced during the rollout of the first two generations of the Web, do we repeat the same mistakes with **IoT**?

# Reinventing the wheel, but an inverted one

One reason for what we discussed in the previous section might be the dissonance between management and engineers. While management knows how to manage known risks, they don't know how to measure them in the field of **IoT** and computer communication. This makes them incapable of understanding the consequences of architectural decisions made by its engineers. The engineers in turn might not be interested in focusing on risks, but on functionality, which is the fun part.

Another reason might be that the generation of engineers who tackle **IoT** are not the same type of engineers who tackled application development on the Internet. Electronics engineers now resolve many problems already solved by computer science engineers decades earlier. Engineers working on **machine-to-machine (M2M)** communication paradigms, such as industrial automation, might have considered the problem solved when they discovered that machines could talk to each other over the Internet, that is, when the message-exchanging problem was solved. This is simply relabeling their previous **M2M** solutions as **IoT** solutions because the transport now occurs over the IP protocol. But, in the realm of the Internet, this is when the problems start. Transport is just one of the many problems that need to be solved.

The third reason is that when engineers actually re-use solutions and previous experience, they don't really fit well in many cases. The old communication patterns designed for web applications on the Internet are not applicable for **IoT**. So, even if the wheel in many cases is reinvented, it's not the same wheel. In previous paradigms, publishers are a relatively few number of centralized high-value entities that reside on the Internet. On the other hand, consumers are many but distributed low-value entities, safely situated behind firewalls and well protected by antivirus software and operating systems that automatically update themselves. But in **IoT**, it might be the other way around: publishers (sensors) are distributed, very low-value entities that reside behind firewalls, and consumers (server applications) might be high-value centralized entities, residing on the Internet. It can also be the case that both the consumer and publisher are distributed, low-value entities who reside behind the same or different firewalls. They are not protected by antivirus software, and they do not autoupdate themselves regularly as new threats are discovered and countermeasures added. These firewalls might be installed and then expected to work for 10 years with no modification or update being made. The architectural solutions and security patterns developed for web applications do not solve these cases well.

# Knowing your neighbor

When you decide to move into a new neighborhood, it might be a good idea to know your neighbors first. It's the same when you move a **M2M** application to **IoT**. As soon as you connect the cable, you have billions of neighbors around the world, all with access to your device.

What kind of neighbors are they? Even though there are a lot of nice and ignorant neighbors on the Internet, you also have a lot of criminals, con artists, perverts, hackers, trolls, drug dealers, drug addicts, rapists, pedophiles, burglars, politicians, corrupt police, curious government agencies, murderers, demented people, agents from hostile countries, disgruntled ex-employees, adolescents with a strange sense of humor, and so on. Would you like such people to have access to your things or access to the things that belong to your children?

If the answer is no (as it should be), then you must take security into account from the start of any development project you do, aimed at **IoT**. Remember that the Internet is the foulest cesspit there is on this planet. When you move from the M2M way of thinking to **IoT**, you move from a nice and security gated community to the roughest neighborhood in the world. Would you go unprotected or unprepared into such an area? **IoT** is not the same as **M2M** communication in a secure and controlled network. For an application to work, it needs to work for some time, not just in the laboratory or just after installation, hoping that nobody finds out about the system. It is not sufficient to just get machines to talk with each other over the Internet.

# Modes of attack

To write an exhaustive list of different modes of attack that you can expect would require a book by itself. Instead, just a brief introduction to some of the most common forms of attack is provided here. It is important to have these methods in mind when designing the communication architecture to use for **IoT** applications.

# Denial of Service

A **Denial of Service (DoS)** or **Distributed Denial of Service (DDoS)** attack is normally used to make a service on the Internet crash or become unresponsive, and in some cases, behave in a way that it can be exploited. The attack consists in making repetitive requests to a server until its resources gets exhausted. In a distributed version, the requests are made by many clients at the same time, which obviously increases the load on the target. It is often used for blackmailing or political purposes.

However, as the attack gets more effective and difficult to defend against when the attack is distributed and the target centralized, the attack gets less effective if the solution itself is distributed. To guard against this form of attack, you need to build decentralized solutions where possible. In decentralized solutions, each target's worth is less, making it less interesting to attack.

# Guessing the credentials

One way to get access to a system is to impersonate a client in the system by trying to guess the client's credentials. To make this type of attack less effective, make sure each client and each device has a long and unique, perhaps randomly generated, set of credentials. Never use preset user credentials that are the same for many clients or devices or factory default credentials that are easy to reset. Furthermore, set a limit to the number of authentication attempts per time unit permitted by the system; also, log an event whenever this limit is reached, from where to which credentials were used. This makes it possible for operators to detect systematic attempts to enter the system.

# Getting access to stored credentials

One common way to illicitly enter a system is when user credentials are found somewhere else and reused. Often, people reuse credentials in different systems. There are various ways to avoid this risk from happening. One is to make sure that credentials are not reused in different devices or across different services and applications. Another is to randomize credentials, lessening the desire to reuse memorized credentials. A third way is to never store actual credentials centrally, even encrypted if possible, and instead store hashed values of these credentials. This is often possible since authentication methods use hash values of credentials in their computations. Furthermore, these hashes should be unique to the current installation. Even though some hashing functions are vulnerable in such a way that a new string can be found that generates the same hash value, the probability that this string is equal to the original credentials is miniscule. And if the hash is computed uniquely for each installation, the probability that this string can be reused somewhere else is even more remote.

# Man in the middle

Another way to gain access to a system is to try and impersonate a server component in a system instead of a client. This is often referred to as a **Man in the middle (MITM)** attack. The reason for the middle part is that the attacker often does not know how to act in the server and simply forwards the messages between the real client and the server. In this process, the attacker gains access to confidential information within the messages, such as client credentials, even if the communication is encrypted. The attacker might even try to modify messages for their own purposes.

To avoid this type of attack, it's important for all clients (not just a few) to always validate the identity of the server it connects to. If it is a high-value entity, it is often identified using a certificate. This certificate can both be used to verify the domain of the server and encrypt the communication. Make sure this validation is performed correctly, and do not accept a connection that is invalid or where the certificate has been revoked, is self-signed, or has expired.

Another thing to remember is to never use an unsecure authentication method when the client authenticates itself with the server. If a server has been compromised, it might try to fool clients into using a less secure authentication method when they connect. By doing so, they can extract the client credentials and reuse them somewhere else. By using a secure authentication method, the server, even if compromised, will not be able to replay the authentication again or use it somewhere else. The communication is valid only once.

# Sniffing network communication

If communication is not encrypted, everybody with access to the communication stream can read the messages using simple sniffing applications, such as Wireshark. If the communication is point-to-point, this means the communication can be heard by any application on the sending machine, the receiving machine, or any of the bridges or routers in between. If a simple hub is used instead of a switch somewhere, everybody on that network will also be able to eavesdrop. If the communication is performed using multicast messaging service, as can be done in UPnP and CoAP, anybody within the range of the **Time to live (TTL)** parameter (maximum number of router hops) can eavesdrop.

Remember to always use encryption if sensitive data is communicated. If data is private, encryption should still be used, even if the data might not be sensitive at first glance. A burglar can know if you're at home by simply monitoring temperature sensors, water flow meters, electricity meters, or light switches at your home. Small variations in temperature alert to the presence of human beings. Change in the consumption of electrical energy shows whether somebody is cooking food or watching television. The flow of water shows whether somebody is drinking water, flushing a toilet, or taking a shower. No flow of water or a relatively regular consumption of electrical energy tells the burglar that nobody is at home. Light switches can also be used to detect presence, even though there are applications today that simulate somebody being home by switching the lights on and off.

> If you haven't done so already, make sure to download a sniffer to get a feel of what you can and cannot see by sniffing the network traffic. Wireshark can be downloaded from `https://www.wireshark.org/download.html`.

# Port scanning and web crawling

Port scanning is a method where you systematically test a range of ports across a range of IP addresses to see which ports are open and serviced by applications. This method can be combined with different tests to see the applications that might be behind these ports. If HTTP servers are found, standard page names and web-crawling techniques can be used to try to figure out which web resources lie behind each HTTP server. CoAP is even simpler since devices often publish well-known resources. Using such simple brute-force methods, it is relatively easy to find (and later exploit) anything available on the Internet that is not secured.

To avoid any private resources being published unknowingly, make sure to close all the incoming ports in any firewalls you use. Don't use protocols that require incoming connections. Instead, use protocols that create the connections from inside the firewall. Any resources published on the Internet should be authenticated so that any automatic attempt to get access to them fails.

Always remember that information that might seem trivial to an individual might be very interesting if collected en masse. This information might be coveted not only by teenage pranksters but by public relations and marketing agencies, burglars, and government agencies (some would say this is a repetition).

# Search features and wildcards

Don't make the mistake of thinking it's difficult to find the identities of devices published on the Internet. Often, it's the reverse. For devices that use multicast communication, such as those using UPnP and CoAP, anybody can listen in and see who sends the messages. For devices that use single-cast communication, such as those using HTTP or CoAP, port-scanning techniques can be used. For devices that are protected by firewalls and use message brokers to protect against incoming attacks, such as those that use XMPP and MQTT, search features or wildcards can be used to find the identities of devices managed by the broker, and in the case of MQTT, even what they communicate.

You should always assume that the identity of all devices can be found, and that there's an interest in exploiting the device. For this reason, it's very important that each device authenticates any requests made to it if possible. Some protocols help you more with this than others, while others make such authentication impossible.

XMPP only permits messages from accepted friends. The only thing the device needs to worry about is which friend requests to accept. This can be either configured by somebody else with access to the account or by using a provisioning server if the device cannot make such decisions by itself. The device does not need to worry about client authentication, as this is done by the brokers themselves, and the XMPP brokers always propagate the authenticated identities of everybody who send them messages.

MQTT, on the other hand, resides in the other side of the spectrum. Here, devices cannot make any decision about who sees the published data or who makes a request since identities are stripped away by the protocol. The only way to control who gets access to the data is by building a proprietary end-to-end encryption layer on top of the MQTT protocol, thereby limiting interoperability.

In between the two resides protocols such as HTTP and CoAP that support some level of local client authentication but lacks a good distributed identity and authentication mechanism. This is vital for **IoT** even though this problem can be partially solved in local intranets.

# Breaking ciphers

Many believe that by using encryption, data is secure. This is not the case, as discussed previously, since the encryption is often only done between connected parties and not between end users of data (the so-called end-to-end encryption). At most, such encryption safeguards from eavesdropping to some extent. But even such encryption can be broken, partially or wholly, with some effort.

Ciphers can be broken using known vulnerabilities in code where attackers exploit program implementations rather than the underlying algorithm of the cipher. This has been the method used in the latest spectacular breaches in code based on the OpenSSL library. To protect yourselves from such attacks, you need to be able to update code in devices remotely, which is not always possible.

Other methods use irregularities in how the cipher works to figure out, partly or wholly, what is being communicated over the encrypted channel. This sometimes requires a considerable amount of effort. To safeguard against such attacks, it's important to realize that an attacker does not spend more effort into an attack than what is expected to be gained by the attack. By storing massive amounts of sensitive data centrally or controlling massive amounts of devices from one point, you increase the value of the target, increasing the interest of attacking it. On the other hand, by decentralizing storage and control logic, the interest in attacking a single target decreases since the value of each entity is comparatively lower. Decentralized architecture is an important tool to both mitigate the effects of attacks and decrease the interest in attacking a target. However, by increasing the number of participants, the number of actual attacks can increase, but the effort that can be invested behind each attack when there are many targets also decreases, making it easier to defend each one of the attacks using standard techniques.

# Tools for achieving security

There are a number of tools that architects and developers can use to protect against malicious use of the system. An exhaustive discussion would fill a smaller library. Here, we will mention just a few techniques and how they not only affect security but also interoperability.

## Virtual Private Networks

A method that is often used to protect unsecured solutions on the Internet is to protect them using **Virtual Private Networks** (**VPNs**). Often, traditional **M2M** solutions working well in local intranets need to expand across the Internet. One way to achieve this is to create such **VPNs** that allow the devices to believe they are in a local intranet, even though communication is transported across the Internet.

Even though transport is done over the Internet, it's difficult to see this as a true **IoT** application. It's rather a **M2M** solution using the Internet as the mode of transport. Because telephone operators use the Internet to transport long distance calls, it doesn't make it **Voice over IP** (**VoIP**). Using **VPNs** might protect the solution, but it completely eliminates the possibility to interoperate with others on the Internet, something that is seen as the biggest advantage of using the **IoT** technology.

# X.509 certificates and encryption

We've mentioned the use of certificates to validate the identity of high-value entities on the Internet. Certificates allow you to validate not only the identity, but also to check whether the certificate has been revoked or any of the issuers of the certificate have had their certificates revoked, which might be the case if a certificate has been compromised. Certificates also provide a **Public Key Infrastructure (PKI)** architecture that handles encryption. Each certificate has a public and private part. The public part of the certificate can be freely distributed and is used to encrypt data, whereas only the holder of the private part of the certificate can decrypt the data.

Using certificates incurs a cost in the production or installation of a device or item. They also have a limited life span, so they need to be given either a long lifespan or updated remotely during the life span of the device. Certificates also require a scalable infrastructure for validating them. For these reasons, it's difficult to see that certificates will be used by other than high-value entities that are easy to administer in a network. It's difficult to see a cost-effective, yet secure and meaningful, implementation of validating certificates in low-value devices such as lamps, temperature sensors, and so on, even though it's theoretically possible to do so.

# Authentication of identities

Authentication is the process of validating whether the identity provided is actually correct or not. Authenticating a server might be as simple as validating a domain certificate provided by the server, making sure it has not been revoked and that it corresponds to the domain name used to connect to the server. Authenticating a client might be more involved, as it has to authenticate the credentials provided by the client. Normally, this can be done in many different ways. It is vital for developers and architects to understand the available authentication methods and how they work to be able to assess the level of security used by the systems they develop.

Some protocols, such as HTTP and XMPP, use the standardized **Simple Authentication and Security Layer (SASL)** to publish an extensible set of authentication methods that the client can choose from. This is good since it allows for new authentication methods to be added. But it also provides a weakness: clients can be tricked into choosing an unsecure authentication mechanism, thus unwittingly revealing their user credentials to an impostor. Make sure clients do not use unsecured or obsolete methods, such as `PLAIN`, `BASIC`, `MD5-CRAM`, `MD5-DIGEST`, and so on, even if they are the only options available. Instead, use secure methods such as `SCRAM-SHA-1` or `SCRAM-SHA-1-PLUS`, or if client certificates are used, `EXTERNAL` or no method at all. If you're using an unsecured method anyway, make sure to log it to the event log as a warning, making it possible to detect impostors or at least warn operators that unsecure methods are being used.

Other protocols do not use secure authentication at all. MQTT, for instance, sends user credentials in clear text (corresponding to `PLAIN`), making it a requirement to use encryption to hide user credentials from eavesdroppers or client-side certificates or pre-shared keys for authentication. Other protocols do not have a standardized way of performing authentication. In CoAP, for instance, such authentication is built on top of the protocol as security options. The lack of such options in the standard affects interoperability negatively.

## Usernames and passwords

A common method to provide user credentials during authentication is by providing a simple username and password to the server. This is a very human concept. Some solutions use the concept of a **pre-shared key** (**PSK**) instead, as it is more applicable to machines, conceptually at least.

If you're using usernames and passwords, do not reuse them between devices, just because it is simple. One way to generate secure, difficult-to-guess usernames and passwords is to randomly create them. In this way, they correspond more to pre-shared keys.

One problem in using randomly created user credentials is how to administer them. Both the server and the client need to be aware of this information. The identity must also be distributed among the entities that are to communicate with the device. In the case of XMPP, this problem has been solved, as described in *Chapter 6, The XMPP Protocol*. Here, the device creates its own random identity and creates the corresponding account in the XMPP server in a secure manner. There is no need for a common factory default setting. It then reports its identity to a Thing Registry or provisioning server where the owner can claim it and learn the newly created identity. This method never compromises the credentials and does not affect the cost of production negatively.

Furthermore, passwords should never be stored in clear text if it can be avoided. This is especially important on servers where many passwords are stored. Instead, hashes of the passwords should be stored. Most modern authentication algorithms support the use of password hashes. Storing hashes minimizes the risk of unwanted generation of original passwords for attempted reuse in other systems.

# Using message brokers and provisioning servers

Using message brokers can greatly enhance security in an **IoT** application and lower the complexity of implementation when it comes to authentication, as long as message brokers provide authenticated identity information in messages it forwards.

In XMPP, all the federated XMPP servers authenticate clients connected to them as well as the federated servers themselves when they intercommunicate to transport messages between domains. This relieves clients from the burden of having to authenticate each entity in trying to communicate with it since they all have been securely authenticated. It's sufficient to manage security on an identity level. Even this step can be relieved further by the use of provisioning, as described in *Chapter 6*, *The XMPP Protocol*.

Unfortunately, not all protocols using message brokers provide this added security since they do not provide information about the sender of packets. MQTT is an example of such a protocol.

# Centralization versus decentralization

Comparing centralized and decentralized architectures is like comparing the process of putting all the eggs in the same basket and distributing them in many much smaller baskets. The effect of a breach of security is much smaller in the decentralized case; fewer eggs get smashed when you trip over. Even though there are more baskets, which might increase the risk of an attack, the expected gain of an attack is much smaller. This limits the motivation of performing a costly attack, which in turn makes it simpler to protect it against. When designing IoT architecture, try to consider the following points:

- Avoid storing data in a central position if possible. Only store the data centrally that is actually needed to bind things together.

- Distribute logic, data, and workload. Perform work as far out in the network as possible. This makes the solution more scalable, and it utilizes existing resources better.

- Use linked data to spread data across the Internet, and use standardized grid computation technologies to assemble distributed data (for example, SPARQL) to avoid the need to store and replicate data centrally.

- Use a federated set of small local brokers instead of trying to get all the devices on the same broker. Not all brokered protocols support federation, for example, XMPP supports it but MQTT does not.

- Let devices talk directly to each other instead of having a centralized proprietary API to store data or interpret communication between the two.
- Contemplate the use of cheap small and energy-efficient microcomputers such as the Raspberry Pi in local installations as an alternative to centralized operation and management from a datacenter.

# The need for interoperability

What has made the Internet great is not a series of isolated services, but the ability to coexist, interchange data, and interact with the users. This is important to keep in mind when developing for **IoT**. Avoid the mistakes made by many operators who failed during the first Internet bubble. You cannot take responsibility for everything in a service. The new Internet economy is based on the interaction and cooperation between services and its users.

## Solves complexity

The same must be true with the new **IoT**. Those companies that believe they can control the entire value chain, from things to services, middleware, administration, operation, apps, and so on, will fail, as the companies in the first Internet bubble failed. Companies that built devices with proprietary protocols, middleware, and mobile phone applications, where you can control your things, will fail. Why? Imagine a future where you have a thousand different things in your apartment from a hundred manufacturers. Would you want to download a hundred smart phone apps to control them? Would you like five different applications just to control your lights at home, just because you have light bulbs from five different manufacturers? An alternative would be to have one app to rule them all. There might be a hundred different such apps available (or more), but you can choose which one to use based on your taste and user feedback. And you can change if you want to. But for this to be possible, things need to be interoperable, meaning they should communicate using a commonly understood language.

## Reduces cost

Interoperability does not only affect simplicity of installation and management, but also the price of solutions. Consider a factory that uses thousands (or hundreds of thousands) of devices to control and automate all processes within. Would you like to be able to buy things cheaply or expensively? Companies that promote proprietary solutions, where you're forced to use their system to control your devices, can force their clients to pay a high price for future devices and maintenance, or the large investment made originally might be lost.

Will such a solution be able to survive against competitors who sell interoperable solutions where you can buy devices from multiple manufacturers? Interoperability provides competition, and competition drives down cost and increases functionality and quality. This might be a reason for a company to work against interoperability, as it threatens its current business model. But the alternative might be worse. A competitor, possibly a new one, might provide such a solution, and when that happens, the business model with proprietary solutions is dead anyway. The companies that are quickest in adapting a new paradigm are the ones who would most probably survive a paradigm shift, as the shift from **M2M** to **IoT** undoubtedly is.

# Allows new kinds of services and reuse of devices

There are many things you cannot do unless you have an interoperable communication model from the start. Consider a future smart city. Here, new applications and services will be built that will reuse existing devices, which were installed perhaps as part of other systems and services. These applications will deliver new value to the inhabitants of the city without the need of installing new duplicate devices for each service being built. But such multiple use of devices is only possible if the devices communicate in an open and interoperable way. However, care has to be taken at the same time since installing devices in an open environment requires the communication infrastructure to be secure as well. To achieve the goal of building smart cities, it is vitally important to use technologies that allow you to have both a secure communication infrastructure and an interoperable one.

# Combining security and interoperability

As we have seen, there are times where security is contradictory to interoperability. If security is meant to be taken as exclusivity, it opposes the idea of interoperability, which is by its very nature inclusive. Depending on the choice of communication infrastructure, you might have to use security measures that directly oppose the idea of an interoperable infrastructure, prohibiting third parties from accessing existing devices in a secure fashion.

It is important during the architecture design phase, before implementation, to thoroughly investigate what communication technologies are available, and what they provide and what they do not provide. You might think that this is a minor issue, thinking that you can easily build what is missing on top of the chosen infrastructure. This is not true. All such implementation is by its very nature proprietary, and therefore not interoperable. This might drastically limit your options in the future, which in turn might drastically reduce anyone else's willingness to use your solution.

The more a technology includes, in the form of global identity, authentication, authorization, different communication patterns, common language for interchange of sensor data, control operations and access privileges, provisioning, and so on, the more interoperable the solution becomes. If the technology at the same time provides a secure infrastructure, you have the possibility to create a solution that is both secure and interoperable without the need to build proprietary or exclusive solutions on top of it.

## Summary

In this final chapter, we presented the basic reasons why security and interoperability must be contemplated early on in the project and not added as late patchwork because it was shown to be necessary. Not only does such late addition limit interoperability and future use of the solution, it also creates solutions that can jeopardize not only yourself your company and your customers, but in the end, even national security. This chapter also presented some basic modes of attack and some basic defense systems to counter them.

As this chapter concludes the book, the reader should now be able to create solutions with **IoT** that are interesting, secure, and interoperable. If you review the solutions proposed in this book, you will notice how many of them solve the challenges presented in this chapter. It is my desire to thank you for your time in reading this book and also to wish you best of luck in your future endeavors.

# Index

## Symbol

**10-foot interface application**
  about 176
  viewing 186, 187

## A

**abstraction model**
  using 191, 192
**actuator project**
  CoAP, adding 98
  creating 22
  hardware 22
  hardware, interfacing 23, 24
  HTTP support, adding 54
  MQTT support, adding 115
  XMPP support, adding 151
**additional security layer**
  connection, maintaining 145
  friendship recommendations, handling 142
  friendships, negotiating 146
  interrupted negotiations, continuing 148
  presence subscription requests,
    handling 147, 148
  provisioning 136-138
  provisioning server interface,
    initializing 142
  provisioning server, searching for 143, 144
  public thing, updating 140
  registry information, providing 145
  requests, handling 143
  thing, claiming 140
  thing, disowning 141
  thing, registering 139
  Thing Registry interface, initializing 138
  thing, removing from registry 140
**authentication** 209

## B

**Bidirectional streams Over Synchronous HTTP (BOSH)** 131

## C

**camera project**
  actions, executing 87, 88
  configurable properties, adding 30, 31
  creating 27
  current settings, working with 32
  devices, discovering 85
  events, receiving 86, 87
  events, subscribing 86
  hardware 27, 28
  hardware, interfacing 29
  initialization 32, 33
  persistent default settings, creating 30
  serial port on Raspberry Pi, accessing 29
  services, discovering 85
  settings, persisting 31
  UPnP, setting up 84
  using 84
  XMPP support, adding 152, 153
**CanBeAddedTo() method** 196
**CanTakeNewNode() method** 196
**class, for actuator**
  control operations, customizing 175, 176
  creating 175
**class, for camera**
  creating 176

class, for sensor
  best class, finding 172, 173
  creating 172
  incoming sensor data, interpreting 174, 175
  sensor data, subscribing to 173
Clayster abstraction model
  about 193
  basics 193
  common data sources 195, 196
  communication, handling with devices 197
  editable data sources 193, 194
  editable objects 194, 195
  key properties, overriding 196
  methods, overriding 196
Clayster.AppServer.Infrastructure
    library 165
Clayster.HomeApp.MomentaryValues
    module 166
Clayster libraries
  about 14
  Clayster.Library.Abstract library 165
  Clayster.Library.Data 14
  Clayster.Library.EventLog 14
  Clayster.Library.Installation library 165
  Clayster.Library.Internet 14
  Clayster.Library.IoT 14
  Clayster.Library.Language 14
  Clayster.Library.Math 14
  Clayster.Library.Meters library 165
  Clayster.Library.RaspberryPi 14
Clayster Management Tool (CMT) 169
Clayster.Metering.Xmpp module 166
Clayster platform
  about 164
  Clayster module, creating 166
  Clayster system, configuring 168, 169
  data sources, browsing 170, 171
  downloading 164
  executing, from Visual Studio 168
  management tool, using 169, 170
  package manifest, using 167, 168
  references, adding 165
  service, executing 167
  service project, creating 165
  URL 164

CoAP
  about 89-91
  development tools, finding 91
  unencrypted version 90
  URL, for interoperability server 91
CoAP, adding to actuator
  about 98
  output, controlling 101, 102
  simple control resources, defining 99
  URL, parsing 100
CoAP, adding to sensor
  about 91
  data readout resources, registering 94
  event notification, triggering manually 93
  JSON, returning 96
  plain text, returning 96
  resources, defining 92
  resources, discovering 97
  resources, testing 98
  XML, returning 95
CoAP gateway architecture
  about 198-200
  diagrammatic representation 199
CoapGetDigitlOutputTxt method 100
CoAP, using in controller
  about 102
  control actions, performing 104
  notifications, receiving 103, 104
  observable resources, monitoring 102, 103
communication, handling with devices
  about 197
  devices, configuring 198
  devices, reading 198
communication patterns 129
Constrained Application Protocol. See CoAP
Constrained RESTful Environments (CoRE)
    Link Format document 97
Content-Type header 36
control application
  application class, creating 178
  application references 180
  binary signal, displaying 182, 183
  brieflets, defining 180, 181
  completing 185
  configuring 186

controller, initializing 178
control rules, adding 179
creating 176
gauge, displaying 181, 182
rendering 177
rendering pipeline 177
updates, pushing to client 184, 185
controller project
  CoAP, using 102
  control states, calculating 26, 27
  creating 24
  HTTP support, adding 60
  MQTT support, adding 118
  sensor data, parsing 25
  sensor values, representing 25
  XMPP support, adding 153
Copper (Cu) 91
custom views 177

# D

Datagram Transport Layer Security (DTLS) 90
Denial of Service (DoS) attack 203
device description document
  creating 67, 68
  device type, selecting 68
  friendly name 69
  icons, adding 69
  references, adding to services 70
  relative URL, providing for web presentation page 71
  Unique Device Name (UDN), specifying 69
Device Description Document (DDD) 66
devices, interfacing with XMPP
  about 171
  class, creating for actuator 175
  class, creating for camera 176
  class, creating for sensor 172
dialog reference 180
Digital Living Network Alliance (DLNA) 65
DigitalOutput class 16
Distributed Denial of Service (DDoS) attack 203
Domain Name System (DNS) servers 37
dynamic link library (DLL) file 165

# E

Efficient XML Interchange (EXI) 129
ExecuteParameterPopupCommand() method 197
ExecuteParameterPopupQuery() method 197
ExecuteSimplePopupCommand() method 197
Export method 20
Extensible Messaging and Presence Protocol. *See* XMPP

# G

General Event Notification Architecture (GENA) 66
GetDisplayableTypeName() method 196
GetIconResourceName() method 196
GetParametersForCommand() method 197
GetParametersLocked() method 197
GetPopupCommands() method 197
GPIO pins
  about 14
  reference link 15

# H

Hardware Abstraction Layer (HAL) 14
hardware, actuator project
  about 22
  interfacing 23, 24
hardware, camera project
  about 27, 28
  interfacing 29
hardware, sensor project
  infrared motion detector 15
  interacting with 16, 17
  interfacing 17
  LEDs 15
  light sensor 15
  SCL and SDA pins 15
  temperature sensor 15
HTTP
  about 35
  basics 36-38
  making binary 90

**HTTP support, adding to actuator**
  about 54
  alarm output, accessing 57
  collective access, to outputs 57
  individual outputs, accessing 56, 57
  REST web service interface, using 59
  test form, using 58
  web services resource, creating 55, 56
  WSDL, accessing 59
**HTTP support, adding to controller**
  about 60
  actuator, controlling 63
  control thread, creating 62, 63
  events, subscribing 60, 61
**HTTP support, adding to sensor**
  about 38, 39
  data export, testing 53
  events, adding for enhanced network performance 54
  graphics, generating dynamically 46-51
  HTTP server, setting up 39-41
  HTTPS server, setting up 41, 42
  measured information, displaying in HTML page 44, 45
  readout request, interpreting 52
  root menu, adding 42, 43
  sensor data resources, creating 51, 52
  user authentication 53
**Hypertext Transfer Protocol.** *See* **HTTP**
**Hypertext Transfer Protocol Secure (HTTPS)** 37

# I

**Internet Engineering Task Force (IETF)** 126
**Internet of Things (IoT)**
  about 11, 163, 189
  Clayster platform 164
  risks 201
  selecting 164
**Internet Protocol (IP)** 37
**interoperability**
  combining, with security 213, 214
  complexity, solving 212
  cost, reducing 212, 213
  devices, reusing 213
  need for 212
  new services, allowing 213
**IoT platform**
**IoT projects**
  about 11
  actuator 11, 22
  bridge 11
  camera 11, 27
  controller 11, 24
  sensor 11, 12

# J

**Jabber ID (JID)** 127
**JavaScript Object Notation (JSON)** 39
**just in time (JIT)** 188

# L

**local area networks (LANs)** 37

# M

**machine to machine (M2M) communication** 35
**Man in the middle (MITM) attack** 205
**media access control (MAC) addresses** 37
**menu reference**
  about 180
  custom menu reference 180
  dynamic selection reference 180
  standard menu reference 180
**message brokers**
  using 211
**Message Queue Telemetry Transport protocol.** *See* **MQTT protocol**
**modes of attack**
  about 203
  chipers, breaking 207, 208
  credentials, guessing 204
  Denial of Service (DoS) 203, 204
  Man in the middle (MITM) attack 205
  network communication, sniffing 205, 206
  port scanning 206
  search features 207
  stored credentials, accessing 204
  web crawling 206
  wildcards 207

MQTT protocol
  about 107
  architecture 109
  publish/subscribe pattern 108
MQTT support, adding to actuator
  about 115
  content, decoding 117, 118
  content, parsing 117, 118
  events, subscribing to 115, 116
  published content, receiving 116
  topic content, initializing 115
MQTT support, adding to controller
  about 118
  actuator, controlling 120
  alarm output, controlling 121, 122
  events, handling from sensor 118
  LED output, controlling 120, 121
  sensor events, subscribing to 120
  sensor values, decoding 119
  sensor values, parsing 119
MQTT support, adding to sensor
  about 110
  content, publishing 113, 114
  MQTT server, connecting to 112, 113
  significant events, flagging 111, 112
  thread life cycle, controlling 110, 111
Multi-Purpose Internet Mail Extensions
    (MIME) 51

# N

Namespace property 196
non-visible services 177

# O

object database 18

# P

ParallelDigitalInput class 16
ParallelDigitalOutput class 16
port scanning 206
pre-shared key (PSK) 210
properties and methods, Clayster
    abstraction model
  commands, publishing 197
  overriding 196

  properties, publishing 197
  structure 196
protocol bridging 190, 191
Public Key Infrastructure (PKI)
  about 37
  architecture 209
publish/subscribe pattern
  about 38, 108
  message broker 108
  publisher 108
  subscriber 108

# R

references, control application
  dialog reference 180
  menu reference 180
Representational State Transfer (REST) 38
Resource Description Framework
    (RDF) 38, 39
risks
  about 201
  managing 202
  neighborhood, knowing 203
root device 66
rosters 129

# S

Secure Sockets Layer (SSL) 37
security tools
  about 208
  authentication 209
  centralization, versus
      decentralization 211, 212
  encryption 209
  message brokers, using 211
  provisioning servers, using 211
  user credentials 210
  VPNs 208
  X.509 certificates 209
sensor project
  Clayster libraries 14
  CoAP, adding 91
  creating 12
  data, persisting 18
  hardware 15

hardware, interacting with 16, 17
hardware, interfacing 17
HTTP support, adding 38, 39
MQTT support, adding 110
Raspberry Pi, preparing 13
sensor data, exporting 19-21
sensor data values, external representation 19
sensor data values, internal representation 18
XMPP support, adding 149
Serial Clock Line (SCL) 15
Serial Data Line (SDA) 15
Service Control Protocol Description (SCPD) 67, 81
service description document
　actions, adding 72
　creating 71
　state variables, adding 72, 73
　unique device name, adding 73
service-oriented architecture (SOA) 38
SetParameterLocked()method 197
Simple Authentication and Security Layer (SASL) 127, 209
Simple Mail Transfer Protocol (SMTP) 126
Simple Object Access Protocol (SOAP) 38
Simple Service Discovery Protocol (SSDP) 66
SoftwarePwm class 16
Still Image service
　actions, adding 83
　evented state variables, initializing 81
　implementing 81
　service properties, adding 83
　web service properties, providing 82
SubscribeToEvents method 86
subscription identity (SID) 86

# T

TagName property 196
Terse RDF Triple Language (TURTLE) 38, 39
Thing Registry 139
Transmission Control Protocol (TCP) connection 37
Transport Layer Security (TLS) 37, 127

# U

Uart class 16
Uniform Resource Locator (URL)
　about 36
　structure 36
Unique Device Name (UDN) 69
Unique Resource Identifier (URI) 38
Universal Plug and Play (UPnP)
　about 65, 66
　device capabilities, documenting 66
　service architecture, providing 66
　service capabilities, documenting 67
Universal Product Code (UPC) 69
UPnP interface
　creating 74
　network, notifying 78, 79
　placeholders, replacing 76, 77
　searches, responding 79, 80
　support for SSDP, adding 77
　UPnP resources, registering 75

# V

Virtual Private Networks (VPNs) 208
Voice over IP (VoIP) 208

# W

web applications 176
web-based CoAP test tool
　URL 91
web crawling 206
web interface
　providing 73
Web Service Definition Language (WSDL) 59
Web Services Description Language (WSDL) 38
web services resource 55

# X

XMPP
　about 125, 171
　additional security layer, adding 136
　basics 126
　communication, authorizing 128

communication patterns 129, 130
extending 130, 131
global identity, providing 127
global scalability, federating for 126
online presence, sensing 128, 129
security, provisioning 132
server, connecting to 131, 132
XML, using 129

**XMPP Extension Protocols (XEPs)** 130

**XMPP implementation** 161, 162

**XMPP Standards Foundation (XSF)** 130

**XMPP support, adding to actuator**
about 151
controller server interface, adding 151, 152

**XMPP support, adding to camera** 152, 153

**XMPP support, adding to controller**
about 153
camera client interface, setting up 157
camera image, fetching over XMPP 157
controller client interface,
    setting up 155, 156
incoming sensor data, handling 154, 155
peer capabilities, identifying 158
peer presence, reacting 159, 160
rule changes, detecting 160
sensor client interface, setting up 153
sensor data, subscribing to 153, 154

**XMPP support, adding to sensor**
about 149
contacts, publishing 150
event subscriptions, updating 149
sensor server interface, adding 149

**XMPP support, adding to thing**
about 133
connection state events, monitoring 134
friends, notifying 135
HTTP requests, handling 135
XMPP network, connecting to 133, 134

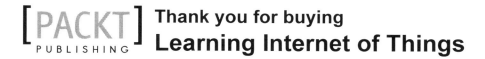

# About Packt Publishing

Packt, pronounced 'packed', published its first book, *Mastering phpMyAdmin for Effective MySQL Management*, in April 2004, and subsequently continued to specialize in publishing highly focused books on specific technologies and solutions.

Our books and publications share the experiences of your fellow IT professionals in adapting and customizing today's systems, applications, and frameworks. Our solution-based books give you the knowledge and power to customize the software and technologies you're using to get the job done. Packt books are more specific and less general than the IT books you have seen in the past. Our unique business model allows us to bring you more focused information, giving you more of what you need to know, and less of what you don't.

Packt is a modern yet unique publishing company that focuses on producing quality, cutting-edge books for communities of developers, administrators, and newbies alike. For more information, please visit our website at www.packtpub.com.

# Writing for Packt

We welcome all inquiries from people who are interested in authoring. Book proposals should be sent to author@packtpub.com. If your book idea is still at an early stage and you would like to discuss it first before writing a formal book proposal, then please contact us; one of our commissioning editors will get in touch with you.

We're not just looking for published authors; if you have strong technical skills but no writing experience, our experienced editors can help you develop a writing career, or simply get some additional reward for your expertise.

## Internet of Things with the Arduino Yún

ISBN: 978-1-78328-800-7    Paperback: 112 pages

Projects to help you build a world of smarter things

1. Learn how to interface various sensors and actuators to the Arduino Yún and send this data in the cloud.
2. Explore the possibilities offered by the Internet of Things by using the Arduino Yún to upload measurements to Google Docs, upload pictures to Dropbox, and send live video streams to YouTube.
3. Learn how to use the Arduino Yún as the brain of a robot that can be completely controlled via Wi-Fi.

## Cloning Internet Applications with Ruby

ISBN: 978-1-84951-106-3    Paperback: 336 pages

Make your own TinyURL, Twitter, Flickr, or Facebook using Ruby

1. Build your own custom social networking, URL shortening, and photo sharing websites using Ruby.
2. Deploy and launch your custom high-end web applications.
3. Learn what makes popular social networking sites such as Twitter and Facebook tick.

Please check **www.PacktPub.com** for information on our titles

## Building a Rich Internet Application with Vaadin [Video]

ISBN: 978-1-78328-892-2   Duration: 02:19 hrs

Easily create powerful, modern web apps with this rich Java framework

1. An iterative approach to building Vaadin applications, taking you from first steps to a complete app.
2. Use navigation and CSS to create a complete web application.
3. Learn how to develop custom widgets and components with Vaadin.

## ExtGWT Rich Internet Application Cookbook

ISBN: 978-1-84951-518-4   Paperback: 366 pages

80 recipes to build rich Java web apps on the robust GWT platform, with Sencha ExtGWT

1. Take your ExtGWT web development skills to the next level.
2. Create stunning UIs with several layouts and templates in a fast and simple manner.
3. Enriched with code and screenshots for easy and quick grasp.

Please check **www.PacktPub.com** for information on our titles

Printed in Poland
by Amazon Fulfillment
Poland Sp. z o.o., Wrocław